Cultural Schizophrenia

D1598362

Modern Intellectual and Political History
of the Middle East
Mehrzad Boroujerdi, *Series Editor*

Cultural Schizophrenia

Islamic Societies
Confronting the West

Daryush Shayegan

Translated from the French
by John Howe

Syracuse University Press

First Syracuse University Press Edition 1997
97 98 99 00 01 02   6 5 4 3 2 1

First published as *Le Regard Mutilé: Schizophrénie culturelle: pays
traditionnels face à la modernité* by Editions Albin Michel, Paris, 1989

Copyright © Editions Albin Michel

First published by Saqi Books, 1992.

Translated into English with the financial assistance of the Ministère
Français Chargé de la Culture.

The paper used in this publication meets the minimum requirements
of American National Standard for Information Sciences—Permanence
of Paper for Printed Library Materials, ANSI Z39.48-1984. ∞™

Library of Congress Cataloging-in-Publication Data
Shayegan, Darius.
        [Regard mutilé. English]
        Cultural schizophrenia : Islamic societies confronting the West /
Daryush Shayegan ; translated from the French by John Howe. — 1st
Syracuse University Press ed.
        p.   cm. — (Modern intellectual and political history of the
Middle East)
        Originally published: Le regard mutilé : Schizophrénie culturelle.
Paris : Albin Michel, 1989.
        Reprint of 1992 ed. published by Sāqī Books.
        Includes index.
        ISBN 0-8156-0507-2 (pbk. : alk. paper)
        1. Middle East—Civilization.   2. Religion and sociology—Middle
East.   3. Islam—Social aspects—Middle East.   4. Religion and
culture—Middle East.   I. Title.   II. Series.
DS57.S4913   1997
956.94—dc21   97-25572

Contents

Foreword

Cultural Schizophrenia is an essay on the mental distortions afflicting those civilizations that have remained on the sidelines of history and played no part in the festival of changes. Although this work owes its existence to my personal experience in the world of Iranian Islam, I believe that its scope extends beyond this world and applies (to some extent at least) to most of the civilizations whose mental structures are still rooted in Tradition and have difficulty in adapting to modernity.

We who were born on the periphery are living through a time of conflict between different blocs of knowledge. We are trapped in a fault-line between incompatible worlds, worlds that mutually repel and deform one another. If accepted consciously, lucidly, without resentment, this ambivalent situation can be enriching; it can amplify the registers of our learning and broaden our sensibility. But the same ambivalence, when sheltered from the critical field of knowledge, causes mental blocks and lacunae, mutilates perceptions and (in the manner of a broken mirror) fragments realities and mental images alike.

The real tenor of this experience, in its current critical phase, hardly impinges on the Western consciousness. For the truth is that it is not a Western problem. The only people really qualified to draw attention to it are those who pay the price, in 'unhappy consciousness.'

Behind these displacements can be seen the outlines of two antagonistic modes of being, two very different historical experiences; but, in spite of their underlying disparities, these are still two faces of humanity's single, common experience in the world. Any hope of a future dialogue between the inhabitants of the planet will depend largely on the outcome of this critical confrontation between two worlds.

Preface

Cultural Schizophrenia is in a way the continuation of my book, *Qu'est-ce qu'une revolution religieuse?* (What is a religious revolution?), which was published in Paris in 1982. In that book my aim was to show the great structures of traditional world vision and their systematic destruction by modern thought—a process that I called "The Fundamental Breach." I depicted the distortions of political discourse in a world where religion, because of discrepancies between conflicting world-views and the hegemony of inevitable Westernization, has been fatally reduced to ideology; hence the phenomenon of ideologisation of Tradition and the false consciousness that results from this state of affairs.

In *Cultural Schizophrenia*, these same themes were studied not on a political level but from an individual standpoint. That is why the conceptual articulations of this book refer back to the existential problems of man. The first chapter commences with the narration of a hypothetical "I," who could be anyone. Progressively this narrative ego reveals his inner contradictions, his state of *In-between*, as if he were caught living in different periods of time, but also as if he had missed the crucial moments of history, like the Renaissance, the Classical period, and the XIX century.

In this work as in the previous one, I had to create new tools of conceptualization, which for the most part were hitherto unknown: the notions of unconscious Westernization, the field of distortions, the idea of superimposition or grafting etc. For instance, the same distortion can be translated as false consciousness on a political level and at the same time be interpreted as cultural schizophrenia on an individual plane. The conceptual distortions are themselves the consequences of epistemological cleavages. They often translate the unbridgeable gulf between ideas and modes of being—divorces which can have devastating effects on human behavior.

In recapitulating the various stages that lead to these distortions, I note that we are situated on the fault-line between incompatible worlds —between two heterogeneous paradigms. I further suggest that in this conflicting situation the two paradigms meet and, like two reflecting screens face to face, disfigure each other by disintegrating their mutual images. Finally, I observe that in this battle of paradigms, there is no doubt that the most recent one—modernity in its broad sense but contaminated with the magical content of tradition—has the upper hand. Why? Because, incorporated into our perceptual apparatus, it has become, whether we like it or not (indeed we are seldom aware of it), the *a priori* form of our vision, the lens that colors our perception of the world.

The last part of *Cultural Schizophrenia* treats the sociological aspects of these distortions. In Book IV, called "The Social Foundations of the Distortions," I have taken into consideration four social categories: the Intellectuals, the Ideologues, the Technocrats, and the Clergy, the latter referred to here as "Strategists of God." The relationships between these categories are explained on the basis of conflicts which oppose Myth to Reason. If the intellectual, as Sartre once declared, is "the unhappy consciousness" of society, a person who desperately tries to avoid the identity of myth and reason by remaining suspended on the razor's edge of non-identity, the Ideologue, on the contrary, is a thinker who *remythologizes* the byproducts of reason, those concepts devoid of all metaphysical content. As for the Technocrat, he is, in this context, the symbol of reason in the service of production, an instrumentalized reason, in which concepts emptied of their content have become simple formal envelopes.

So whatever their respective functions, all these categories personify distortions that float in the mental and social spaces of our world. The main ambition of this book is to bring out, as much as possible, these discrepancies and to sensitize the reader to the pernicious effects of these distortions. Whether I have succeeded in shedding some light on these subjects is another matter. The numerous reactions that the publication of this book evoked and its subsequent translation into several languages, suggest that perhaps I have struck, somewhere, a sensitive chord.

Book I

The Split[*]

* This section first appeared in *Le Débat*, no. 42, Nov.–Dec. 1986 (Gallimard, Paris).

1
Postponing the End, so Unable to Begin

The influence of the West and the modernity which underpins it have led to the appearance of multiple centres of resistance in the contemporary Islamic world. One reaction is a regression towards original mythology, in the hope that it will resolve in miraculous fashion all the moral sufferings and social inequalities that afflict these societies; another is a *fuite en avant* into increasingly perilous adventures; yet another, a categorical refusal to accept the challenges posed by the new age. Each of these rather perverse expedients expresses a different facet of the same phenomenon and, whatever their apparent differences, they are all symptoms of the same profound malaise. In my opinion this malaise results from the non-comprehension, or non-assimilation, of a major historical phenomenon: modernity in its broadest sense. This has never been confronted for what it is, objectively, in terms of its philosophic content, but always in terms of its traumatic impact on our traditions, our ways of living and thinking. As a result, ever since the earliest contacts, attitudes to modernity have been complicated by a moral component: either admiring, as when, during the first contacts with the material power of the Occident, the Islamic world discovered to its great astonishment how backward it was, and what an enormous gulf separated it from Europe; or maleficent when, later on, shutting itself off from European influence, it strove to revive its own most deranged hallucinations. The first reaction could not have been more enthusiastic; the second, on the other hand, borrowed the hysterical language of obsessional rejection. In both cases, the West was never considered as a new *paradigm* providing a break with the past, possessing its own laws and its own logic of domination, but rather as a conspiracy of occult forces using their material power to take possession of us, shake us to our very foundations, debauch our morals, corrupt our virtues and reduce us by degrees to a state of political and cultural slavery.

It is true that the first Islamic thinkers of the *Nahda* (renaissance) had the merit of paying particular attention to the political and juridical systems of Europe. They were strongly attracted by the notion of individual rights and liberties. Nevertheless one essential escaped the earliest thinkers, as it does most of their present-day successors: these basic ideas, whose qualities were so admired, were not the results of some recent miracle, but the end-product of an exceptional historical process — almost, I would say, the product of a paradigm shift — and could not be transplanted into our world without displacing and marginalizing the traditional values to which we were so attached, and which occupied every corner of our public space.

Besides, these new ideas, revolutionary in many ways, cleared the way to other layers of reality and created other social relations, most of which had not existed in our closed traditional world. For in the religious and totalizing perspective provided by our vision of the world, these realities — if they were noticed at all — were either found to be absent or thought to result from the material contingency of things. Referring to the spirit of the Arabic language, Jacques Berque rightly observes, 'The Arabic tongue, whose every word leads to God, has been designed to conceal reality, not to grasp it.'[1] The tension between the unveiling of new zones of reality and the atavistic compulsion to exclude or eject them from the field of knowledge was bound to create fissures in the consciousness: although things were changing externally, mental projections still functioned according to the old mode of representation. How were people to live with these internal chasms? Whether we like it or not, this is still the insoluble problem underlying all the mental distortions — and they are very numerous — that ravage our world. The problem can only be raised by people born into these civilizations. Just as no person can stand in for another in the act of dying, so nobody from a different

4

civilization can experience existentially this split in the interior of his or her soul. It is, in other words, our own specific and inalienable destiny.

In the interests of clarity, I will allow myself a digression at this point. Let us imagine a hypothetical individual clamped in the jaws of this split and wrestling with a contradictory double fascination: the enchanted vision of a world still infused with the aura of collective memory, and the equally compelling allure of the new and unknown. Such a person would feel strongly alienated, both by the shock of the radical changes affecting him and by a pervasive nostalgia (made doubly poignant by the progressive withdrawal from the world stage of the universe to which it refers, leaving everywhere the signs of its imminent disappearance). This hypothetical individual would reason more or less as follows:

The new ideas assailing me, the new objects I see ranged before me in all their depth and solidity, are wholly alien to me. I have neither appropriate words, nor adequate mental imagery, to understand them properly. They are something inaccessible surging suddenly into my field of knowledge. It is true that I perceive them, that I make use of them, that I exercise command over them as well as having to endure them, but somehow they remain apart, suspended in abeyance amid the flux of my memory. I cannot trace their genesis, nor was I present at their birth. I played no part in the succession of crises which preceded their fabrication, or in the modes of production which made them possible. They are strange, outlandish things that I cannot avoid, things that upset my habits and constrain me in inescapable ways. But there is something in them which I find seductive, which attracts me, something whose support I can hardly do without, even by making every effort. All my mental categories have been fashioned to hide what is now being revealed in the world I live in; my thought functions differently, uncovering zones of being which run counter to the logic of the things around me. Somehow my thought unveils the *suprareality* of the things it considers, while veiling their concrete reality. What it veils is what touches me directly; what it unveils, by contrast, is what is no longer there. For the suprareality with which the thing is invested is now absent from my world, having been swept away in the torrent of changes.

My vision of the world refers back to an original transfiguration which suffused everything in a climate of magic. The world of objects, the world in which they exist and from which they derive their functions, does not have the same solid reality for my mind as it does in the eyes of someone who conceived and experienced it. I inhabit a world of absence: my thought is concerned with ideas which have no hold on reality. Internal content and external forms are no longer linked organically. Any ideas that start to take shape are soon twisted by contact with the deformities which ravage parts of my natural ecology. The 'delay' between what I project and what is there before me represents, not just a chronological dislocation, but an ontological divide. Objects have changed a lot more quickly than my perceptions of reality. The changes have scrambled my references, tangled my route-maps, but they have not modified the deeper zones of my psyche. My tendency to 'mythologize' reality is such that I believe much more firmly in the unchanging essences of a substantial vision than in the historical process of the evolution of things.

There is a void which I cannot fill in the content of my representations, trailing far behind the industrial productions which surround me on all sides. This yawning gap is not just a difference in mode of life, but a change in my mode of perception. My thought has been sheltered from the great shocks of history. In the West, revolutions caused by scientific and technical upheavals produced paradigm shifts which moulded consciousness to the imperatives of each new way of looking. This has not occurred in my case. My consciousness is still rooted in a world of enchantment. It is true that, as a result of continual bombardment, I am susceptible to the irresistible attraction of new things; but their genealogy and archaeology remain unknown to me. New ideas strike me with full force, stamp their imprints on my mind leaving indelible traces, but hardly manage to alter the content of a memory which refers stubbornly to its own genealogy. I know that times have changed, that the world has been transformed, that history unceasingly shapes new modes of production and new social relations; but the content of this history was formed in my absence. I am no more familiar with its genesis than I am responsible for its results. All I know is that this new world has an implacable logic, that it imposes its ready-made structure upon me, and that I can neither influence its course nor retrace the road it followed to reach the place in which I now find myself.

And by the way, where, strictly speaking, am I? My historical co-ordinates are altogether different. I do not calculate in terms of centuries, sixteenth, seventeenth or eighteenth; or in terms of the historical breaks which mark the transition from the Middle Ages to the Renaissance, or distinguish classical from modern periods. The sequence of historical periods means nothing to me. I tend to scramble the order of the centuries, because the qualitative discontinuities which punctuate

Western history have no concrete representation in my mind. I have a past which — because I continually refer to and resuscitate it — is confused with the present; and a present which is my future. It is true that over the last hundred years I have experienced profound upheavals, that I talk about history, think about it, do my best to understand its mechanisms and linkages, to get back to the very relative sources of my pseudo-modernity. But during this short period, which marks my formal entry to a time of ever-broadening horizons, on the psychic level I have continued to inhabit a meta-history in which the *before* and the *after* are confused with the *after* and with *post-history*. And between the two, I find myself postponing an End without which there can be no Beginning.

When I attempt to recall the great poets — so important to a Persian like myself — I do not see them as successive portraits displayed in the gallery of time. A poet is not associated with a period through the calendar or through the atmosphere of his time, a classical poet predating a romantic, a symbolist coming later, and so on; no, all are linked together with the invisible centre of memory, which seems to invest all of them with a timeless aura, so that they become as it were the luminous rays of a single sun. Each great poet is an interlocutor co-present in the dimension of time which he describes: the time of epics, the mystical time of return to the inner self, the fragmented time of parenthetical moments like flashes of reality. I thus exist in a constellation where each poet follows his own elliptical orbit around my totalizing vision. That is why I see in pictures, express myself in sonorous rhythms, think in poetry. I cannot tell them apart in terms of periods and eras. Of course, the critical and historical studies launched at the beginning of the century conveyed the basic idea; I do discern different styles, changes to language, semantic modifications. But everything indicates that the fundamental problem remains immutable. The great theme of 'national identity' which preoccupied the poet Ferdowsi in the tenth century is still real for the late twentieth-century thinker struggling to restore cultural nationalism in the face of assaults from religious obscurantism. The ideals which inspired a fourteenth-century mystic are still present, proportionally speaking, in the disenchanted look I cast on the faithlessness of the world. A discredited monarch is instinctively likened to the tyrant Yazid who foully shed the blood of the Imam Hussein; when his successor turns the country into a cemetary full of dead martyrs he is said to resemble Zahhak, the evil sovereign of the *Shahnameh*, or *Book of Kings*, who demanded the daily sacrifice of the brains of innocent children to feed the serpents growing from his shoulders. One might say that the mythical structure of reality is unchanging, that the characters vary over time but are always found to be playing the same roles; a Manichaean struggle between Shades and Light in the relentless repetition of cycles.

When I commune with the mainstream of my culture I find no breaks with the past, no changes of direction, no deviation from its great guiding principles. There is something which survives all changes, something which always sails serenely above the harshness of the times, as if God were tirelessly repeating the same familiar litanies. Within range of this transmitter, lines of demarcation and qualitative distinctions appear artificial, synthetic, not connected in a meaningful way with the eternal course of events. Yet I cannot help knowing that, despite my dependence on this state of things, despite the persistence of problems supposedly solved for all time, there have somehow appeared insidious gaps and flaws which alter both the intact image I have composed of myself and the one I have always attributed to the real world. I sense in a confused way that there is a hiatus between what I have inherited from my forebears and what has become of the world. Nothing in my culture has prepared me for it, nor was there any warning of a change of this order. Yet there is this *hurt* inside my mind, inside the confused order of things which long ago escaped my control.

I learn at school all the conventional subjects that constitute the intellectual baggage of modern man. I study mathematics, science, history, geography, literature; but where does it come from, all this fragmented knowledge taught out of context, without organic links to the cultural canons of my tradition? Where did I get the Cartesian *cogito*, the transcendental ego, the movement of the Being incarnated in time, the neutral objectivity boasted by the scientific method? Am I still in the Middle Ages? Did I experience the classical age and the epistemological breaks of the modern age? Was I decomposed in the corrosive acid of the age of criticism? Was I shaped by the bourgeois values of capitalism? Am I ripe for the world revolution (supposing it to be possible)? These are the questions that crowd my mind; for my personality tends to seek comparisons, concordances of time and place. Like it or not, I am evolving in a comparative world. I no longer live in a closed self-sufficient universe; I am importuned by the other, if only through the influence he brings to bear on me without my knowledge. I reason through comparisons, through extrapolations, through a sequence of affiliations. I profit from the exemplary models offered by the museum of history; I try to apply them to my own destiny. More than this, I seek to reconstruct my own past to conform to the standards imposed on me by birth, by definition, as a matter of course. This wish to see myself through the eyes of others is so strong, so firmly anchored in the established modes of my judgement, that I re-evaluate my entire past in the light of criteria which come from outside. When I try to reconstruct the broad lines of my recent history — for example, the passage from the Constitutional movement (1905-11) to the founding of the nation state (1926) in Iran — I find myself introducing notions which only correspond in the most tenuous way with the singular process that actually took place. When I talk about the role of the bourgeoisie, I forget that this notion has precise connotations in a particular culture, and that my use of the expression hardly entitles me to assume its existence as a sociological fact. Most of the ideas I borrow have little or no counterpart in social reality. The overblown excess of the hollow speeches I find so intoxicating manages, just about, to cover up my conceptual shortcomings.

So comprehension of my history is falsified from the start: it operates on criteria which relate to my true problems only in the most tenuous fashion. Wherever I look within myself, I see only the boring repetition of the same eternal themes, the same refrains, the same sterile slogans, moving ceaselessly about like fugitive dunes across the unchanging desert sand. And the same answers always come up in reply to the same questions. As if, however far I travelled, I were fated always to arrive back at the same starting-point.

What connection is there between the frenetic technology of a world nothing can stop and the visionary passivity of my own teachers of thought? What link between Hegel and Ibn Arabi, Kant and Sohravardi? What possible relationship is there between the invitation to make the most incredible journeys and this retreat into oneself, this inability to see anything of the world except what one wants to see: an aura transfigured by the magic of sublime illusions! While those who shaped my thought advise me to absent myself from this world in order to be more present in the other, my modern teachers advise me on the contrary to accept nothing which is not verified experimentally, to distrust dogmatic *a priori* assumptions and wish-fulfilment dreams. Schizophrenia is not just something that conditions me in spite of myself; it is maintained by a whole network of signs which come to me from life, from school, from the street, from politics, from the bottomless stupidity which turns my days into an eternity of stunned boredom. Casual untruth has infiltrated the texture of my ideas, it infects my deformed concepts, it smoulders in the inconsistency of my actions and follows me into my inner defences becoming, in a sense, my *second nature*. I am out of alignment with myself, and with what I am supposed to embody, and with what beckons me from all sides. I am racked between new ideas which evaporate for lack of a context and ancient ideas arthritic with the failure to adapt. Lying becomes a way of life, a way of apprehending a reality which evades me, which imposes repeated failures upon me, against which I am defenceless. I am obliged to invent excuses and seek scapegoats: multinational capitalism, the devastating aftermath of colonialism, Zionism, imperialism, any 'ism' you like: they are all just words, mere palliatives for my comfort, sedatives that plunge me deeper into my dogmatic slumber.

I am vaguely aware, however, that to free myself from the tutelage of the idols to which I am still shackled, I must tear away the veil of humbug which protects my illusions from the real world. And that I will need courage to take a leap in the dark, to cut my umbilical cord. I must make this jump at all costs, even (as the poet put it) at the risk of falling into eternity. I must free myself from the vicious circle of excessively simplistic explanations. If things are to change anywhere it must be inside people's heads, all the way from ground level to that of the most acute, the most uneasy consciousness. Attitudes are not changed by modifying infrastructures, but by overturning the minds themselves. I am astonished to find that my problems have not changed since I became aware of my displacement. I ceaselessly repeat the same nostalgic themes, ceaselessly pursue the same scapegoats, retire ceaselessly behind the same barricades; somehow my thought, castrated by secular impotence, operates through threadbare clichés. It is certainly true that the protagonists of the drama change over time, but the dramaturgy itself is unvarying. I am always the victim of the other. My innocence is infallible; every misfortune which afflicts me can be imputed to mysterious forces beyond my control. For to tell the truth I am the victim of a fate as old as the world itself, which keeps reappearing under new disguises: Alexander the Macedonian, the Bedouin Arab, Genghis the horseman of the Steppes, the two-faced Briton, the ugly American, the Soviet Bear and God alone knows what else.

Even so, just give me modern tools, an abundance of petrodollars, the most tolerant ideas of the age of democracy, and in the space of a few months I will set up the most repressive state apparatus in the world: a paradise of hell. I have not lacked for means! I inherited billions, in hard currency, but unfortunately I did not know how to make use of them. No, what I really lack is ideas. Because, you see, I am blocked somehow. A blockage as old as my soul, as tenacious as my *idées fixes*, as pathological as my obsessions, as neurotic as this cumbersome religion I do not know what to do with. And — let us be frank — my thought is totalizing. It is not interested in the specific, the factual. Details fatigue it, precision bores it, criticism discourages it. I am as lazy as a *rentier* who, content with his meagre income, shrinks from risky ventures which might disturb his peace. What I like are plump, straightforward ideas which explain clearly where I come from, where I am going, why I am the lord and master of God's creatures, why I am the Depository of Divine Attributes which make me a potential superman, how I will die (should this eventuality come to pass) and how I will later be reborn as an Angel among the blessed. I love Angel stories and come across them everywhere. One look at the visionary poems of my mystics and I am flying!

It hardly matters whether I am a materialist, a Marxist, even an infidel or atheist. After using the fine blade of Marxist dialectic to carve up my insolent detractors I can go peacefully home, open the *Diwan* of the divine Hafez or the *Mathnawi* of Rumi and get drunk on words and images. At such a moment I am ready to share the banquet of the Angels, to taste the delights of mystic orgies. And even — why not? — to follow the pilgrim birds on their quest for fabulous Simorgh. For, to tell the truth, I play on a risky seesaw between Angel and anti-angel. Not only does this state of things fail to surprise me, not only am I unaware of my own contradictions; I am even shocked and hurt when more experienced minds point them out to me. I take an innocent view of my contradictions. I am no more responsible for them than I am for this accursed revolution which has driven me from my country. I had nothing to do with it. It was a plot by imperialists who grew jealous when they saw us becoming the Japanese of the Middle East. So what next? All is written in the Quran, and history, if it has a meaning at all, is just a pale commentary on that writing. All is written in our heads, and the rest follows, infallibly, by mathematical deduction.

2
On Holiday from History

Let us try to be rational for once! What exactly has been happening over the last four centuries? What has happened since the discovery of the great laws of astronomy? The last phases of the construction of our cathedrals of thought coincide oddly with the rise of Cartesian subjectivity. One is tempted to agree with Hegel that the World-Spirit was deserting the areas where culture had been perfected and was seeking asylum in the West. Why? I have no idea. There have been so many learned explanations on the subject, so many masterly exegeses, that I must spare the reader any more of them. Let us stay with the facts. For more than three centuries we, the heirs of the civilizations of Asia and Africa, have been 'on holiday' from history. (Doubtless there are exceptions.) Having cemented the last stones into place on our Gothic cathedrals of doctrine, we sat back to contemplate our handiwork. We succeeded so well in crystallizing time in space that we were able to live outside time, arms folded, safe from interrogation.

All these fantastic edifices, all these metaphysical doctrines — Iranian, Indian, Chinese — were complete; all the great religious architectures had been erected into gravity-defying temples of contemplation. Drunk with God to the point of ecstasy and self-forgetfulness, we turned everything — land, people, works of art — into ineffable signs of His glory. All His attributes, names, manifestations, caprices, were painstakingly catalogued, then fixed for all time in immutable canons. We analysed His fancies, understood His mysteries, deciphered the hieroglyphic codes of His abstruse language. We became so expert in Divine Science that nothing, nothing at all, was safe from our metaphysical curiosity. Soon we felt as comfortable in the labyrinth of the eternal cosmogonies as in the nooks and crannies of our own houses. The meticulous ritual of our daily acts was ruled by a timetable of divine whims. Every action was transformed into a rite, every discourse into a consecration of His Word. We had integrated Him so perfectly into our lives that we could no longer distinguish between our own private space and that of the Divinity. So it was that God was subjected to our tireless attention, while we remained trapped in the searchlight of His omnipresence.

Having completed our world, we withdrew to enjoy the undisturbed repetition of pious devotional acts. But as we gazed on our works, those cunning little fellows in the West were already working on the ruination of our world. Those enterprising barbarians were deserting their own cathedrals without a backward glance and talking about all kinds of weird things: Copernican revolution, humanism, the difference between faith and knowledge, man as self-sufficient subject, and so on. Things that would have made our hair stand on end if we had had any idea of their appalling consequences. Happily, we were not involved in any of this. Then these infidels started making astonishing objects: cannons, rifles; and soon they were churning up our seas with their improved ships and coming to visit us. Of course we welcomed them with open arms in accordance with the rules of hospitality. We were amazed by their mechanical toys, their technical discoveries, the diabolical ingenuity of their sorcery. Doubtless to their great satisfaction. To us Muslims, beneficiaries of the last Prophecy of the age of Revelations, these barbarians were just infidels; infidels who set out voraciously to learn our languages, to study our customs, to use on us something we heard about only much later: anthropology. We were just another interesting subject for them, like the objects they observed through their telescopes and their instruments.

It never occurred to us that we might do the same thing. Do what, after all? Bury ourselves in pointless concerns like that? Innovate? Break with the Holy Tradition? It would be the height of blasphemy. Anyway, in the final analysis our work was complete; we were already 'on holiday'. We

13

knew exactly where we had come from, where we were going and where we were spending the interval between the beginning and the end of time. And besides, to risk offending the Lord by interfering shamelessly in the natural course of things would have unleashed the forces of evil. We were warned against this danger some twenty-five centuries ago by a Chinese sage:

> When Dsi Gung was passing through the region to the north of the river Han, he saw an old man working in a garden. The old man had dug irrigation channels. He was climbing down into the well and climbing out again with a vessel full of water which he poured into the channels. He was working extremely hard but achieving little.
>
> Dsi Gung said to the old man, 'There is a way of irrigating a hundred channels in one day, so that great results are achieved with little effort. Would you not like to use this method?' The old man stopped working, looked at him and said, 'What would that be, then?'
>
> Dsi Gung said, 'You use a pole of wood, weighted at one end and not at the other. It enables you to draw water in profusion. It is called a chain-well.'
>
> An expression of anger appeared on the face of the old man, and he said with a laugh, 'I have heard my master say that he who uses machines does everything mechanically, and he who does everything mechanically ends with the heart of a machine. Now, he who carries the heart of a machine in his chest loses his innocence. He who has lost his pure innocence becomes uncertain in the movements of his spirit. Uncertainty of spirit cannot agree with the true path. It is not that I am ignorant of these things, but that I would be ashamed to make use of them.'[2]

What the Chinese sage said nearly twenty-five centuries ago would seem perfectly sensible to a Hindu or a Muslim. Perhaps a Muslim would not have used quite such exact terms, but the general idea is still present in his obsessional fear of innovating in any way at all: in the field of thought as well as that of technology. And when you are afraid to innovate, and remain passive in relation to others, you let yourself be had. Which is what, fatally, happened. Came the day when we saw that we had fallen into a trap, that we no longer held the reins of our own destiny, that railway lines divided up our land, telegraph poles criss-crossed our plains, steamships filled our harbours. Our attitude was one of withdrawal: just as we contemplated our monuments, enjoying our secular holidays with impunity, so we settled down to passive scrutiny of these merchants, these missionaries, these expeditionary corps who bustled around us. Our attitude was rather like that of the Persian prime minister who, questioned in parliament about the presence of the Allies in the country during the Second World War, made this historic remark: 'They come and go and have nothing to do with us.'

We were so convinced of our own impotence that we ended by granting these shrewd foreigners the same magical qualities that we used to attribute to the Divinity. The English did it!, we would say. The Russians did it! It's all a plot by the British, the Americans, any secret services you want. When the Shah went, it was because 'they' decided it was time. When the Imam took his place, it was because 'they' had always wanted it so. If I myself went out in the street howling like a man possessed, it is because I was hypnotized by the BBC and manipulated by the CIA. The entire universe was in league to exploit us, persecute us and push us around; while we, bled white by all the knives in our back, sought desperately to get out in one piece. For had we not completed our labour, erected our grandiose monuments, drained to the last drop the ardours of our faith — we, the innocent children of the fall?

Battle-weary, we settled down to consume ideas, objects and methods whose mechanisms we could barely decipher. We understood that in a world dominated by the power of technology our ancient wisdom, like the Chinese gardener's simple vessel, was becoming increasingly obsolete, while our ideas were falling into disuse. As a final illusion, we formed the conviction that it would be possible to be selective with the nature of the things we were obtaining: to separate the wheat from the chaff, to choose technology and firearms while heroically ruling out the subversive, laicizing ideas which lay behind them. To be, in short, fundamentalist Muslims wholly subservient to the omnipresence of *Shari'a*, enterprising capitalists, efficient technocrats and — why not? — ardent nationalists as well. But then, before we had had time to take proper stock and get things in hand, we found ourselves on the wrong side of the stream: between what was happening in the world and what was happening in our heads, an abyss had opened up. Suddenly, the bucolic vacation was over; for in the meantime the world had changed, history had moved on, our familiar ecology had crumbled, and we were left stumbling about in no man's land, neither the land of our forefathers nor that of the new masters. The absentee always gets the blame! That is the way things are. Yes! We were in the wrong, because we had missed our rendezvous with history.

15

3
Some Examples: China and the Islamic World

When the first missionaries landed in China during the reign of the Ming dynasty (1368-1644) they initially adopted a seductive strategy: how, they wondered, could they convert the Chinese without offending their beliefs? The missionaries, who in effect were technocrats long before their time, used the technique of scattering bait for the intellect. For conversion, as later became apparent in all colonized countries, is the phase which precedes occupation. The Chinese were quickly attracted by the science and technology introduced by Italian missionaries like Ruggieri and Ricci, who arrived in South China in 1583. Besides, as Jacques Gernet points out:

> Ricci recognized that he owed a large part of his renown among the educated classes to his map of the world and his scientific teachings (mathematics and astronomy). Science — and also technology — not only drew quite large numbers of literate men to the missionaries, but increased their prestige and their following. This is a point on which supporters and critics of the missionaries are in agreement: the principal success of the *Western Barbarians* came from their calendar methods, from their ability to improve the calendar by using

astronomical instruments, and from the help they gave in gun manufacture[...] They were judged useful to the State and to the defence of the Empire.[3]

The reaction was not slow in coming. The Chinese soon perceived that the campaign of seduction had a two-faced, swindling, ill-intentioned side. In the words of a Chinese writer attempting to expose the Machiavellian manoeuvres of these Jesuits:

> By helping to make guns, they cause people to rejoice in their ardour. By praying for rain, they give the impression that they possess magical techniques. Their clocks, their clavichords, their spyglasses, dazzle with the skill they embody. They win associates by employing the gold they possess in abundance, they disarm people with their extreme politeness.[4]

For behind all these machinations lay the deliberate intention to mislead the Chinese and turn them away from their tradition. Hence the complaints of Chinese sceptics who perceived a campaign on four levels: to bewitch the venal with money, to entice the intelligentsia with scientific knowledge, to dupe the moralistic with moral precepts and to fanaticize the population at large by instilling the fear of hell. Nevertheless the critical attitude of the Chinese remained ambivalent, and we find the same ambivalence throughout history in Oriental peoples subjugated by the technical power of the West but unable to discern the organic connections between religion and science.

The simplest solution for the Chinese, as for most Oriental peoples, was to make a distinction between the technology and its underlying metaphysics: to accept the first which is useful and efficient, while rejecting the second which is baleful and contrary to ancestral tradition. The shrewd Chinese suspected that the missionaries were more or less materialistic for, as an observant writer points out:

> Is it reasonable, under pretext of venerating the Master of Heaven,[5] to declare that Heaven and Earth are without intelligence, that the sun, moon and planets are just brute things, that the gods of the mountains and rivers, the gods of the Soil and the Harvests are devils, and that it is not necessary to make sacrifices to the ancestors?[6]

What this Chinese sage so appositely condemned and what the Jesuits, already secularized in their understanding of nature, professed, is no less than the specific phenomenon that gave birth to Western science: the desymbolization, or as German thinkers called it the disenchantment (*die Entzauberung*), of the world. As we know, this phenomenon was one of the basic premises making it possible to conceive the idea of a profane, quantifiable, mathematically predictable nature. The fact that the universe had been created by a geometrician God permitted the appearance of a mathematical conception of nature, which led in turn to the birth of modern science. Whatever people may claim, classical Western science results largely from the secularization of Christian theology. It also depends on a number of other established views and practices: the distinction between the spiritual and the temporal, between theology and philosophy; the idea of a transcendent personal God, and the subjectivity which corresponds to it; and the crucial idea which brought history into the very heart of creation: the Incarnation. All these things were shocking to the sensibilities of the Chinese, for whom Heaven was bound up with the impersonal order of nature and the Emperor was the Son of Heaven, bearer of its mandate to preserve the harmonious order of the universe. The duality of body and spirit was incomprehensible to them, and the Incarnation patently absurd. 'How can a tortured and executed barbarian be called Master of Heaven?'[7] asks a prosecution text from the Nanking trial of the heterodox association of Christians in 1616-17.

It is sheer illusion to imagine that a technique can be learned without acquiring, or at least understanding, the metaphysical underpinnings which constitute its armature. Nevertheless this illusion has played a part in every attempt to modernize by non-Western civilizations over the past century and more (Japan, of course, excepted). The case of the Islamic world is the most catastrophic of all.

The history of relations between Islam and Christianity is one of simultaneous repulsion and fascination. It is interesting to recall that the Islamic world, which at one time was greatly influenced by Greek thought — witness the translation of Greek philosophical texts into Arabic — ended by rejecting the West and withdrawing into increasingly rigid attitudes. This came about through a number of factors. Initially the reservations about the West were of theological origin. The West has always been associated in the Muslim mind with the Christian religion. The Muslim's messianic conviction that his religion was the last revelation and his Prophet Muhammad the Seal of Prophecy meant that he saw Christianity as a backward, not to say obsolete, religion, and consequently believed Muslims to be superior to Christians in every way. By the time the military expansion of the West and the resounding defeats of the armies of Islam had imposed a new type of relationship, forcing Islam — by now represented by the Ottoman Empire — to bow to the hard reality of Western technical and military superiority, the Muslims' attitudes had become too arthritic to adapt to the new circumstances. The situation was complicated by the dazzling speed and scale of Islam's own expansion back in the seventh and eighth centuries, when in a very short period the Muslims had conquered through holy war vast tracts of territory belonging to the Christian world. The West answered this first Islamic Jihad, from the eleventh century onward, by launching the *reconquista* of the Iberian peninsula and other Christian territories; the second expansion of Islam, notably that of the Ottoman Empire soon after its apogee under Suleiman the Magnificent (1520-66), came face to face with a qualitative change in the European cultural zone: the dawning of the scientific and technical age, to which Islam remained entirely resistant owing to its closed intellectual stance and its vast inertia.

Three major events of European history — the expansion of maritime routes, the Renaissance and the Reformation — remained entirely foreign to the Islamic world. And in a sense these three factors gave birth to the new modernity. The Renaissance and the extraordinary curiosity which resulted from it set the West on the road to the conquest of other cultures, and thus transformed its closed world into an infinite universe. Galileo's mathematization of nature opened the way to the emergence of the natural sciences and their by-products, improved weaponry and shipping. The Reformation freed medieval societies from the yoke of the Church and led to the centralization of power, or in other words the establishment of absolutism. The technologies used, as Fernand Braudel points out in the case of navigation, were not isolated phenomena but linked systems or groups of techniques, for example 'the sternpost rudder, plus the clinker-built hull, plus shipborne artillery, plus ocean navigation'.[8] Although some techniques can be exchanged and diffused fairly easily in isolation, the association or grouping of techniques, the product of a certain scientific vision of the world in conjunction with a certain perception of reality, cannot be transplanted into societies where these qualitative changes have not taken place and are consequently unrepresented in people's minds. This is what happened to the Islamic world.

The consequences of this unprecedented development were the three shocks inflicted on the Ottoman Empire. These three shocks, according to Bernard Lewis, were the defeat of the Ottomans by Russia in 1774, resulting in the treaty of Küçük Kaynarca which granted territorial, political and trade concessions to the Russians; the annexation of the Crimea by Russia in 1783; and, most important of all in its cultural significance, Bonaparte's Egyptian campaign of 1798.[9]

A much greater consequence of this third event was the penetration into the Islamic lands of the new ideas of the French revolution. This was the first movement of ideas in Europe to break through the barrier that had separated the world of the unbelievers from the world of Islam and to exercise a profound effect on Muslim thought and action. One of the reasons for this success, when all previous attempts had failed, is no doubt that the French revolution was secular — the first great social and intellectual upheaval in Europe to find ideological expression in nonreligious terms. Such earlier European movements as the Renaissance, the Reformation, the scientific revolution, and the Enlightenment had passed without effect in the Islamic world, without even being noticed. Perhaps the main reason for this is that all of them were more or less Christian in their form of expression and therefore barred from entry by the intellectual defenses of Islam [. . .] In such a secular or, rather, religiously neutral ideology, Muslims might even hope to find the talisman that would give them the secrets of western knowledge and progress without endangering their own traditions and way of life.[10]

But looked at from any angle, the relations between the West and the Islamic world reveal one undeniable fact: the contrast between the Europeans' growing, ever-improving knowledge of the Muslims (although not necessarily of their mentality or psychological comportment) and the Muslims' ignorance, not to say benighted apathy, where the West was concerned. An example may serve to illustrate this imbalance. By the end of the eighteenth century the Western scholar had access to extensive material on the Islamic world: 'Some seventy books on Arabic grammar had been printed in Europe, about ten for Persian, about fifteen for Turkish. Of dictionaries there were ten for Arabic, four for Persian, and seven for Turkish.'[11] On the other side, there was nothing in Arabic, nothing in Persian and nothing in Turkish either. The first dictionaries appeared in the nineteenth century:

> The first bilingual dictionary of Arabic and a European language by a native Arabic speaker was published in 1828. It was the work of a Christian — an Egyptian Copt — 'revised and augmented' by a French orientalist and, according to the author's preface, was designed for the use of Westerners rather than that of Arabs.[12]

This situation has continued to deteriorate until the present day: although a few inadequate efforts have been made, the great works of Western literature and thought are still largely unavailable in the languages of Islam. Even though some have been translated, the work has been done in such a slipshod and truncated manner that these works have themselves become a source of intellectual pollution and epistemological distortions, not to mention the absence of standardized terminology which, in the case of the human sciences, may turn out to be catastrophic. The result is that an educated Muslim who is not fluent in one of the European languages has strictly no access, not even the most tenuous, to the great creations of the West. The resources offered by his own language are generally limited to the great works of the classical period. Everything that has been thought, written or discovered for several centuries, in the natural sciences as much as the human sciences, can be communicated to him only through translations, most of which are still frankly deplorable.

4
The Fear of Losing Identity

The distinction between a technique which is useful, because effective and a well-spring of power, and a thought which is subversive, because contrary to tradition, became an issue for the Muslims too. Like the Chinese of the Manchu period, they decided to retain the technical contribution while proscribing the metaphysics on which it was based.

A longing for cultural identity? Perhaps. Fear of being short-circuited by dangerous modes of thought? Undoubtedly. Either way, this contorted attitude has not really changed in our time. It is a basically ambiguous approach whose hypocrisy and double language reflect our split personality: both in our scorn for a science we consider materialist but can no longer do without, and in our complacency about an agonizing tradition which is more and more obviously anachronistic in a rapidly evolving world. These half-measures are the product of a situation where nothing is settled by criticism, where everything is left hanging in a miasma of implications, veiled aspirations and unexpressed regrets. Without even being aware of the underlying contradictions, we want to be both modern and archaic, democratic and authoritarian, profane and religious, ahead of the time and behind it. This might have been possible, had we accepted the need for adjustment and separation, albeit only externally, of two modes of life whose incompatibility generates contradictions on all levels. In Japan, for example, where the working environment and the modern life-style are Western while family life and private customs remain traditional, people's normal activities are not paralysed by this compartmented structure, which also protects them from violent upsets.

But Islam is very different. In its fundamentalist form, at least, it makes imperious demands: it wants to rule everything, to manage society, to regiment minds and make them impermeable to the swamping tides of technological mutation. More than this, it tries to make them resistant to research and innovation.

> Fundamental research [Jacques Ruffié tells us] is the royal road of progress; it is the equivalent, in the field of learning, of macrogenesis on the biological level. It is the source of innovation and creativity, and by throwing out new plans ensures the upward progress of human societies.[13]

By halting our cultural progress, fundamentalism — a regressive phenomenon — not only drags us into a new obscurantism which is an affront in itself to our basic common sense, but also blocks our upward progress, given that biological evolution stopped more than forty thousand years ago with the emergence of Cro-Magnon man.

And what is the attitude of the Islamic world's intellectuals to this danger? In a recent book,[14] twenty-four Arab novelists, poets and philosophers from ten different countries ranging from Morocco to Iraq pronounce on the problems of Islam. The essays cover the resurgence of fundamentalism, the present condition of Islamic culture, the upheavals affecting Muslim countries and the likely causes of further disaster. One common denominator is that almost all the authors are firmly opposed to the formation of an Islamic government, arguing that its blind resistance to the mutations of the modern age can only lead to failure. Some, like the Iraqi Abd al-Rahman Mounif and the Palestinian Emile Habibi, believe religion should remain a private matter. The argument is that when religion invades the public domain it is transformed *ipso facto* into a coercive and repressive ideology. Recourse to fundamentalism of any kind (the Iraqi poet Abd al-Wahhab al-Bayati says) is in the final analysis a 'compensation for a lack'; either that or a subterfuge to mask the failures of secularism and nationalism. The point is also made that, by

23

withdrawing into itself and rejecting all change, Islam is stiffening into a congealed state and slowly becoming a sort of Church (the present condition of al-Azhar), very different from the enlightened Islam of the *Nahda*. The Egyptian writer Hussein Amin points out:

> Eighty-five years after Qassem Amin tried in 1899 to settle the question of the veil for women, people are still arguing about it. And there are fewer voices calling for the abolition of the veil today than there were eighty-five years ago.[15]

Another Egyptian, Gamal al-Ghitani, challenges 'any present-day Arab leader to apply the Islam of Omar Ibn al-Khattab'.[16] In other words, how can a model fifteen centuries old be applied to a contemporary society? The Sudanese author Tayeb Salih believes that the idea of a return to the time of the Prophet is pure utopianism. A regression which, incidentally, means an erosion of liberty:

> In 1926 [al-Ghitani writes] when Taha Hussein's book on anti-Islamic poetry was banned, there was a revolution. Just recently a ban was imposed on the *Thousand and One Nights*, and nobody uttered a word in protest.[17]

Yet another Egyptian, Louis Awad, points out that fundamentalists, unlike the people of the *Nahda* who admitted their backwardness and sought ways of extracting Islam from its impasse, consider the West to be morally underdeveloped. While Muhammad Abduh, among others, sees religion as a legitimate weapon of defense, members of Islamic groups regard it as an instrument for the seizure of power. Any turning back is seen as a hindrance to national renaissance. Mohammed Arkoun believes that to return to the sources is to discount the important theological work done in the first four centuries of the Hegira. To attempt such a return is really just a *fuite en avant*, the result of attributing sacred status to the *Shari'a* in the social imagination. Nor has Islam ever amounted to a system of government. In the Umayyad period it was the instrument of a state which can hardly be called Islamic, while the Abbasid caliphate was strongly coloured by a government apparatus of Sassanid (Iranian) rather than Islamic character. The Tunisian writer Mahmoud Messadi finds a happy description of Arab republics which resemble, he says, 'modern Emirates'; and he adds vehemently that to attract the famous return to the roots of Islam is about as realistic as 'expecting to revive disinterred corpses'.[18] The Algerian novelist Rachid Boudjedra says that Islam is totally incompatible with a modern state, citing the Iranian example which represents 'the total, terrible failure of the Islamic system in practice.'[19]

Many of these authors seem to be traumatized by the Iranian revolution, the best living example of what can happen to a religion when it gets too entangled in worldly matters. Another Algerian, Tahar Ouettar, goes so far as to accuse the Americans of making Islam into 'a natural rampart against what they call the red peril'.[20] And the Algerian writer Kateb Yacine not only thinks that Islam can never become a modern state, but wants it purged of the fanatical subcultures which are so helpful to leaderships (who routinely exploit obscurantism to outmanoeuvre one another and counter the forces of progress).

The Moroccan author Abdelkebir Khatibi analyses the place of language and the co-existence of three systems of law (*Shari'a*, customary or common law, and modern law) which share between them the fields of Moroccan society. He believes that, because the very structure of Islamic society is based on dialogue, it can never adapt to a theocratic system of any kind. But he tells us nothing about resolving any contradictions which may arise between one system of law and another. The Tunisian author Abdelwahab Meddeb writes that any fundamentalism which cites an exclusive frame of reference to justify rejection of the other can only be regressive:

> Instead of rejecting Europe, why should Islam not follow some of the Asian peoples and submit to a humble apprenticeship which might enable it to assimilate, and perhaps eventually overtake, this same Europe?[21]

The authors differ on the causes of fundamentalism. The Egyptians and Lebanese are still obsessed with the defeat of 1967 (which incidentally had a much less resounding impact in Iran). The Lebanese writer Youssef al-Khal identifies rising and declining periods in the history of Islam: the ascendant period of the *Nahda* in the nineteenth century, for example, is contrasted with the period of decadence after 5 June 1967. Another Lebanese, Rachid al-Da'if, concentrates on Muslim mental blockages, discerning areas of rigidity caused by people's fear of questioning ancestral certainties; as a result everyone is stuck in the swamp of collective memory, unable to progress, out of touch with reality. The Egyptian novelist Naguib Mahfouz thinks that the roots of fundamentalism go back to the defeat of 1967 and the failure of experiments with liberalism and socialism. Finally Tawfik al-Hakim (also from Egypt) criticizes the 'dusty paraphernalia' of institutional Islam, whose basis in the rhetorical and grammatical disciplines makes it incapable of grasping the spirit of modern science.

But although the reasons for fundamentalism are listed, more or less, few of these authors try to explore the deeper philosophic meaning of Islam's backwardness and the splits generated by it. The fact that in the late twentieth century Islam is still showing interest in long-obsolete utopian solutions (Ideal City), and is ceaselessly repeating the same unanswered questions, shows that something is seriously amiss; that something essential has been left out. Perhaps (as we suggested at the beginning of this work) this discordance with modernity implies a radical incompatibility whose full extent has yet to be measured. Let me explain. Instead of just dumping Islam on top of something with which it is incompatible, might it not be a better idea to remove it from the public domain and relegate it to its proper place: as a culture, certainly a rich one, but only a culture, like all the others which have appeared on the planet? What, after all, is this irreducible specificity claimed by the exclusive upholders of Islam? It could hardly be any more specific than Hinduism for the Hindus, Buddhism for the Buddhists or Shintoism for the Japanese. But in order to realize this, one has first to be aware of the epistemological breaks which marked the advent of the modern age; breaks whose multiple implications in the fields of epistemology, psychology and social science are not, in my opinion, sufficiently understood or discussed. The blockages and blind spots which haunt us, which paralyse us, usually result from our failure to adapt to the realities of the world. I would say that our vision is *fractured* or *scrambled* in relation to reality. The only tools we have which are capable of liberating us internally and effecting a change of register in our very mode of perception are critical thought, and the sharp blade of a fundamental, merciless scrutiny brought to bear on even the most exclusive truths. Without this reflection on the very nature of our civilization and its underlying paradigm, we will always be paddling complacently in the shallows of ambiguous discourse, the sort of thing that occupies the time of certain Islamic thinkers.

A case in point is the Egyptian Abd al-Rahman al-Sharqawi, who draws a distinction between an Islam comprising a priestly caste in the pay of the

[handwritten: evert into Law vs reflect on its guidance principle —]

government, and an innocent Islam based on the values of the Prophet and his cousin and son-in-law Ali. I believe, on the contrary, that any religion erected into a Law governing the state and society must be retrogressive. This has nothing to do with whether the Islam in question is good or bad; it is simply that Islam as a socio-political totality had its day a very long time ago. But this is not to reject the cultural and mystical aspects of the religion. In this respect Islam is undoubtedly an important dimension of the human heritage, just like the other great religions of the world. But to make out (as some do) that the Islam of Ali is still confronting the Islam of the Umayyads, that there is still a crucial choice to be made between Alavid Islam and Safavid (*Shari'ati*) Islam, is to display a Byzantine fussiness which actually obscures reality rather than illuminating it.

The risk of distortions becomes greater still with the elaboration of what Raymond Aron so aptly calls 'a chain of identifications'. Thus al-Sharqawi asserts, for example, that Islam is democratic because it has had *shuras* (a sort of consultative council), citing in support this *hadith*: 'Consult your companions on communal matters.' Another Egyptian, Youssef Idris, goes even further: *[handwritten: who are the companions?]*

> When we examine the content of our cultural heritage we find, intimately mingled with this rich and complex whole, notions and values which are indisputably Islamic; so it may be said that notions and ideals such as socialism, for example, or democracy, have been known here for a very long time, much longer than they have been known in the West.[22]

And Ahmad Baha'eddin adds: 'There is absolutely no contradiction between Islam and democracy.'[23] *[handwritten: (maybe autocracy)]*

My view is that on the contrary there is a contradiction, precisely because of the paradigm shifts which made possible the emergence of a phenomenon like democracy. To try to match two notions which belong to different constellations of ideas, kept apart by the great historical caesuras on which modernity is founded, is to attempt a chain of identification and misread the genealogy of the concepts involved. Between these fundamental notions there are wide fissures which need to be bridged by means different from the ones we usually employ.

Before there could be democracy there had first to be a secularization of minds and institutions; the individual as such had to be an autonomous subject by right, and not an anonymous soul dissolved in the gelatinous mass of the *umma* (the Islamic community); the law had to have a contractual basis; and, finally, the imperious legitimacy of national sovereignty had to take precedence over the coercive repression of dictators or the no less stifling tyranny of the religious authorities. Democracy is the child of the Enlightenment. And the Enlightenment is the apotheosis of the age of criticism: that is to say, coldly objective criticism of dogmatic truths. In the words of Octavio Paz:

> Democracy is not a superstructure, but a popular creation. Moreover, it is the condition, the basis, of modern civilization. Hence, among the social and economic causes that are cited to explain the failure of the Latin American democracies, it is necessary to add the one I mentioned earlier: the lack of a critical and modern intellectual current.[24]

What Paz says about Latin America is even more true of the Islamic world. The absence of this modern and critical intellectual current leads to the use of a double language, permits chains of identification, complacently marries the carp and the rabbit, leads us into a morass of improbable distortions, weaves a network of lies through whose meshes we blithely clamber, without going through the hard apprenticeship in the uses of reason. What Rachid Boudjedra says of modern Arabic literature, that it is 'a Western form thrown roughly over a reality which has nothing Western about it',[25] is equally true in an inverse sense where religion is concerned. Throwing Islam roughly over secular concepts such as democracy, socialism and liberalism results in hybrid mixtures, explosive cocktails which fill minds with confusion rather than helping to solve our problems.

Herein lies the failure of the *Nahda*, as well as that of the *Thawra* (the era of revolutions which began in the 1950s). The people of the *Nahda*, subjugated by the West, never realized that behind Western power lay a changed vision of the world; that between their Islam and modernity lay a deep gulf which could not be bridged by a return to their ancestral values, nor by a reform of the *Shari'a*. What was needed was a change of register, of wavelength; the public domain needed to be swept clear of nostalgic mythologies to make room for the establishment of another perspective, another value system.

The problem of the Islamic world resides in its cumbersome atavisms, its defensive reflexes, its intellectual blockages and above all in the

28

The borderline
state of
Islamic
society
Rigid
Inflexible

illusory pretension that it possesses ready-made answers to all the world's questions. We need to learn a certain humility, a certain understanding of the relativity of values. We have accomplished no more than the Indians, say, or the Chinese. Indeed their civilizations were in many respects more complex, far more elaborate and refined, than our own. The point is not to make comparisons but to acquire a measure of humility and free ourselves from the crazed egocentrism that lets us believe the world begins and ends with Islam. If Islam was once great, it is because at the time of its genesis it was able to assimilate the most diverse elements and melt them together in the crucible of a prodigious synthesis. Remember the multiple influence of Greek, Iranian and Indian elements. Remember, too, the enormous contributions made to Islam's early development by the conquered peoples, whose level of civilization was often greatly superior to that of the Muslims. The current trend towards the proliferation of fundamentalisms of every stripe is not just failing to renew the spirit of Islam; it is turning it into a funeral procession of petrified dreams wandering off to lose itself in the sands of the desert. Fundamentalism prunes intelligence down to the level of emotional and visceral reflex. And any decline in intelligence is a step towards decrepitude.

Book II

The Ontological Displacement[*]

[*] This section first appeared in *Itinérances*, issue entitled 'L'Eveil du coeur' (Warning from the Heart), no. 1, May 1986 (Albin Michel, Paris).

1
Reality is Always Somewhere Else

The inhabitants of our planet do not yet all share the same way of seeing the world. To a Hindu haunted by the irresistible drive of omnipresent divinities, 'myth' is more real than daily life; to a Mahayana Buddhist the life of the Bodhisattva is more luminous and informative than the convoluted, frankly illusory course of history — which in any case is only one of many aspects of the *samsara* (the cycle of rebirth). A Shiite Muslim lives in anticipation of the Coming of the Imam who is to save the world; and if this event is anticipated, in the meantime, by the appearance of a succession of rabid sages, his eschatological certainty remains undisturbed. His entire consciousness is adjusted to blank off reality and discern what seems to be essential on the other side of it. Existence, for him, is not a matter of social relations formed by modes of production, nor the 'thing in itself', nor the absolute Spirit in time. Moreover, anyone attempting to convey these ideas to him in his own language will quickly discover that the task is impossible. There exist neither the concepts, nor the tools, nor the means of communicating them. There is, so to speak, simply no electrical contact between the different ontologies. They are insulated from one another by the historical hiatus; we are protected by our metaphysical 'holiday' against any intrusion into temporal reality by the

Evil One. When we plumb the depths of the Oriental ontologies, we never reach a firm footing like the one Hegel found in the Cartesian *cogito*, but are thrown on the contrary into the abyss of abysses. Look where we will — at the Mystery of Essence in the speculative Islamic mysticism whose illustrious exponents Sohravardi and Ibn Arabi are so attractive to the young; at the void of non-substantiality in Buddhism, at the vertiginous paradoxes of the mysterious Tao — we find nothing, absolutely nothing, to which we can anchor ourselves.

Reality is always somewhere else. It is not even real, since reality if it exists is an illusion pure and simple. What is so confidently called the object has no meaning, it is there as the reflection of something else, the lantern-slide of a suprareality which is never captured in any frame of knowledge. For knowledge exists in the same way as different states of being, different levels of presence. If objectivity is fictitious in this context, the subjectivity behind it is even more so. Man is the centre of things while being nothing. He is everything because he is the jewel of creation, distinct from the other created beings in that he incarnates the divine Logos; but he is nothing, because he is not a founding authority. Everything he is, everything he represents, comes from Another. And this Other in the final analysis is the bottomless foundation of the universe.

But what happened between this ontology of olden times and the one on which the modern age is founded? One thing certainly occurred: there was a *lowering of gaze*. When I say lowering, I do not imply any value judgement. I use the metaphor of height to convey a change of focus from primary contemplation of smudged, distant horizons to sharp scrutiny of the most immediately accessible concrete things. In any case, scientific observation, interest in the specific and particular, the quantitative measurement of objects, found a place in human consciousness only when the lure of metaphysical temptations started to fade.

Heroic act, maybe; Promethean audacity, perhaps; rebellion against established truths, undoubtedly. One is almost tempted to say that the visionary gaze of religious man became the visual gaze of modern man. Suddenly, what had always been before our eyes was discovered anew, stripped of the transfiguring influence of the old way of seeing. It is often said, for example, that the Renaissance discovered the laws of perspective, as if medieval miniaturists had been unable to see what was before their eyes. Of course, they could see it; but they were conscious at the same time of a more 'real', more enchanted dimension, whose ideational content brought it closer to visionary reality than the dimension apparently revealed by visual perception. Between this ideational vision and the perceptive scrutiny of an observer, there is a transmutation of the way of seeing. The disenchantment of this quasi-magical gaze led to the discovery of a quantitative aspect, which eventually reduced the world to geometric extension; and this in turn, at the beginning of the present century, underwent another dazzling metamorphosis to become quantum mechanics.

This reversal of the situation is probably one of the fundamental pillars of modernity. Its effects are as incalculable in the perception of nature, God and humanity as they are in history. In fact the meanings of these four ideas become completely different when they are moved from one ontology to the other. In the West, the effects of this reversal were felt in the passage from the metaphysical to the social, then to history. The problem of evil, for example, remained a metaphysical subject for some modern thinkers like Pascal, but for philosophers of the Enlightenment it became something else. Pascal reproduces all the great Augustinian themes in modern language. Although his method is Cartesian, the double nature of humanity, whose greatness and baseness he catalogues, is seen as a product of the Fall — a mythical event predating the birth of humanity. Therefore man cannot expect to understand his true condition through unaided reason:

Know then, proud man, your own paradox. Down, helpless reason! Silence, futile nature! Learn that man is infinitely beyond the reach of man, and hear from your Master what is your true condition, so far unknown to you. Hearken to God![1]

But Jean-Jacques Rousseau situates the problem elsewhere. He endows humanity's metaphysical double nature with a historical dimension, in which the natural state is contrasted with the cultural state: 'All things are good as they come out of the hands of the Creator, but every thing degenerates in the hands of man.'[2] Thus the problem of responsibility for evil no longer originates from God, or from some sort of fall during prehistory, but arises out of history itself which unceasingly modifies all societies. The solution should therefore be sought in history, not in the mythical dimension of original sin. Man in the natural state is a noble savage, moved by a self-esteem which is his instinct of self-preservation, his natural innocence. He is not yet affected by society which will make him into a selfish and oppressive being, and transform his self-esteem into self-regard. Society alters man's natural character and makes him an alienated being, driven by passions and unsatisfied desires. This alienation is inscribed in the march of progress itself. Every evolution of society is an alienating process. Liberation is no longer to take place through ontological change, but through the renovation of society itself (which will put an end to greed, vanity and exploitation by subordinating individual will to the general will founded on virtue). It is man himself who must become his own saviour by promoting a juster society, where instead of submitting to the arbitrary will of others he would voluntarily obey the general will.

> Such is the solution, [E. Cassirer writes] that Rousseau's *philosophy of law* offers to the problem of theodicy. It is a fact that he situated this problem on entirely new ground, taking it from the metaphysical level to the heart of ethics and poetics.[3]

This 'mental migration' from metaphysics to the different territory of history, and the alienation caused by the progress of economic and social relations, are precisely what distinguishes the West from the other civilizations of the planet. We can say simply that the distance covered in the course of this mental *house-moving* causes a reversal, an inversion of all categories, in the same way that the appearance of the constellations would be altered by a journey over some vast astronomical distance. Between the two poles lies the vacancy of the civilizations which have not made the journey. A move in which can also be found the reason for all the fissures, chasms, rifts and breaks which pull the contemporary world apart, causing social earthquakes and upheavals in international relations and dividing the world into zones which are overdeveloped, or underdeveloped, or both at once.

The situation is rendered even more intractable by the fact that the former state of things does not stay intact, but is contaminated by the planetary diffusion of new modes of thought whose operational efficiency enables them to erode the ancient edifices of the world from the inside. It is the purest fantasy to imagine that there remain any major cultural areas untouched by the successive waves of modernity. It is also the case that any thought of going back, any revival of fundamentalism in any form, is an illusion. Tradition, if it exists at all, cannot get back ontologically to its starting point in the pre-modern period: it is stuck for ever in post-modernity. Apart from a few Amazonian tribes which may have miraculously escaped being massacred by the whites, and perhaps one or two other groups vegetating in God knows what remote backwoods of the planet, all cultures of whatever origin and location have been touched by modernity; that is, by this downward migration of the mind. These days we all live in polyglot zones, fields of skirmish where all outlooks are to be found, those coming from the old vision of things as well as those forged by technology, development and history.

The tower of Babel is a reality, not just where languages are concerned — although there too we have almost insoluble problems — but for mentalities too. Religious delirium, revolutionary obsessions, women's emancipation, regression into increasingly fraudulent utopias, Star Wars and the revival of obsolete beliefs, jostle in a kaleidoscope of opinions, faiths and visions in which nobody knows what he himself is talking about, let alone the premises underlying this or that political discourse. While wishes and hopes still refer to those beliefs most emotionally charged with ancient tradition, the conceptual structures through which they are now articulated are the backward and monstrous spawn of an ill-digested modernity. Interspace, the place between, has become as it were the normal setting of life. Attempts are made to understand, to analyse. But so much effort has to be devoted to explaining the details, to exposing the guilty motives on all sides, that the essential is forgotten. People remain unaware of the historical breaks which turned the West into the stronghold of modernity, and the other civilizations of the world into enormous ancient monuments.

2
Hardening of the Scholastic Arteries

The planet's older civilizations, most notably the great Asian cultures, stopped being creative after the seventeenth and eighteenth centuries. These two centuries were a turning point in the history of the world, the seventeenth dominated by the Cartesian innovation in method, the eighteenth by the Enlightenment and by criticism. Metaphysical duality was reflected politically in the private domain of freedom of conscience and the public domain of absolutist power. By the eighteenth century the private domain was censuring governments and exposing the dialectical contradictions between morality and politics. This gave birth to the idea of crisis and the attempts to moralize power which, as we know, resulted in the ideology of revolution. None of these developments affected the Asian civilizations which continued to drift down the broad stream of their original quest. But their creative energy was flagging, and finally ran out at the dawn of the great changes which were to transform world history; the Asian cultures remained highly resistant to these changes until the second half of the twentieth century.

For example, the great synthesis of Islamic thought in Iran was completed in the seventeenth century, during the reign of the Safavid dynasty (1501–1722). The renaissance of the School of Isfahan, the impressive doctrinal achievement of Molla Sadra Shirazi (1571-1640),[4] brought together a number of convergent currents and fused them together in the crucible of a potent synthesis. Sadra was a contemporary of Descartes; while he was putting the finishing touches to a movement that was secular in many ways, and adding the last stone to the imposing edifice of Islamic metaphysics, Descartes was short-circuiting the past and hacking out new avenues which were going to make humanity into the founding authority of the universe. All subsequent developments in Iranian thought have been, in a sense, commentaries on Sadra's *oeuvre*, whose metaphysical content will never be surpassed. For once that synthesis was in place, erected vertically like a Gothic arch, innovation was possible only if accompanied by a break with the premises of Islamic theology: something a religious outlook can tolerate only by denying itself. The result was a sort of log-jam of thought, the renewal of a *prophetic philosophy* repeated over and over again, under all circumstances, by one thinker after another, leading to severe hardening of the scholastic arteries. This became more apparent as the Western influence, first felt in the late eighteenth century and growing stronger over the next hundred years, circulated new ideas — mainly social and political — which these civilizations were not equipped to deal with in any way. Beleaguered by these increasingly aggressive modes of thought, the societies responded by turning inwards and marginalizing themselves; meanwhile, individuals lived out and mimetically reproduced their ancestral social comportment, thinking in outmoded patterns which grew daily more out of step with the changing realities of the outside world.

The Indian civilization which had assembled vast metaphysical edifices, prestigious cathedrals of thought, over more than three thousand years, began to run out of breath in the seventeenth century: just like Iranian thought, just like Chinese culture. India in fact was one of the most radiant centres of civilization in the heart of Asia. Its role in Asia can be likened to that of Greece in the West. Hinduism expanded gradually to include all the philosophic mutations and new ideas which emerged on the fringes of brahmanic orthodoxy; and ended by absorbing them all into its vast melting-pot, with the exception of Buddhism and Jainism which were excluded for rejecting the sacred authority of the Vedas. Buddhism, one of the most universal creations of the Indian genius, was primarily an export religion. The lamp of wisdom lit by the Buddha in the sixth century BC illuminated large areas of mainland Asia and spread the basic categories of Indian civilization throughout the Far East;

there, in contact with other civilizations equally brilliant, they underwent astonishing metamorphoses and contributed to prodigious syntheses.

S. Radhakrishnan[5] identifies four periods in Indian philosophy: the Vedic period (1500-600 BC), the Epic period (600 BC-AD 200), the period of the *sutras*, and the Scholastic period which ended in the seventeenth century. Over more than three millennia, from the Vedic period to the end of the Scholastic era, we can trace the progressive enrichment of a vision of the world which emerges from the mythological songs of the Vedas, and later sets into the rigid sacrificial doctrine of the *Brahmanas*, only to leap back into flashing life with the *Upanishads*. According to Hindu tradition the Vedic *Upanishads* are the works of great *Rishis* (seers) of ancient times, who withdrew into the silence of the forest and described, in somewhat esoteric verses, a metaphysical experience in which the mind awakens to the investigation of prime causes; the ritual of sacrifice is internalized, making human breath into the ultimate offering; and the quest for the Absolute, formulated as the total identification of man with the universe — *tat tvam asi* (thou art that) —, acquires a vertiginous, almost obsessional dimension.

On the fringes of brahmanic orthodoxy (and in reaction to it, especially among the *kshatriya* or warrior caste), there appeared all sorts of audacious, heterodox doctrines: questioning the authority of the Vedas, denying that the world had foundations and substituting the void, like the Buddhists; subscribing to a strictly relativist logic, like Jainism; professing a dualistic cosmology like the *samkhya*; celebrating the cult of Vishnu (Vasudeva Krishna) or Shiva (Pashupati), leading respectively to the establishment of Vishnuite and Shivaite doctrines; even — like the materialist *carvakas* and the *lokayatas* — denying all transcendence and accepting nothing that was not palpably real.

All but the most eccentric of these doctrines appear in the great epic the *Mahabharata*, in which the incarnation of Vishnu in the form of Krishna is accompanied by highly developed philosophic and theological teachings, for example the doctrine of *samkhya-yoga* in the *Bhagavad Gita*. The great epic thus constitutes an encyclopaedia of all the ideas and beliefs which were later canonized in writings of disconcerting concision.

All the schools of thought accepted by brahmanism were fixed in very short texts called *sutras* (brief, very condensed formulations easily consigned to memory). It seemed appropriate to comment on the *sutras*, then write commentaries on the commentaries, then commentaries on the commentaries on the commentaries, and so on. This whole literature of commentaries, which are often very tedious but of great technical rigour, constitutes the Scholastic period. During it there appeared on the Hindu side great commentator–thinkers like Shankara, Ramanuja, Vacaspati Mishra, Vijñana Bhikshu; and on the Buddhist side, audacious thinkers like Nagarjuna, Ashvaghosha and Buddhaghosha. This period saw an extraordinary development of Indian thought, a sort of ornate Gothic skyscraper with an architectonic structure unprecedented in the history of civilization (but which ended by suffocating under its own weight). From the seventeenth century onwards, Hinduism was out of breath: there would be no more creation, only repetition, mannerism and eventually sclerosis.

Alongside this last development, however, another very important spiritual phenomenon shone with its own special brilliance: India's relations with Islam, which were due mainly to the reign of the Mughal dynasty. Babur, sovereign of Kabul and a descendant of Tamerlane, had overthrown the Lodi dynasty to found the famous Mughal Empire in 1556. Under Babur's grandson Akbar there began the most prestigious era in India's recent history.

The reign of Akbar (1542-1605), considered in several ways to be the golden age of Indo-Islamic relations, initiated a period of great literary activity. The Islamic culture of the Mughals was mainly Persian-speaking, with Persian the official language of government and the vehicle of Islamic cultural and religious values; indeed those Iranian poets, painters and thinkers who were obliged to flee Safavid fanaticism at home found a haven at the court of the Mughal sovereigns, and were able to settle in without any cultural discomfort. Persian remained the official language until 1857 (the date of the Sepoy rebellion or 'Indian Mutiny') when, by an act of 1858, the Indian subcontinent was integrated into the British Empire, inaugurating an English administration of colonial type. One of the most significant achievements of the Mughal era was the translation of Sanskrit classics into Persian, an event which ranks in importance with the translation of Greek texts into Syriac and then Arabic, or of Arabic texts into Latin at Toledo in the middle of the twelfth century.

What can only be called teams of translators were formed with the help of the best minds of the age: Fayzi the 'Prince of Poets', his brother Abol Fazl, a historian and government minister, and others. In this way, among many other works, were translated the *Mahabharata*, the *Ramayana*, the *Bhagavad Gita*, the *Atharvaveda* and the *Pañcatantra*. The spirit of syncretism faded under Akbar's successor Jahangir (1569-1627) but shone out once more under the influence of the imperial prince Dara Shokuh (1615-59), who had inherited his great-grandfather's keen interest in Hinduism and comparative religion. The *Sirr-e Akbar* (Greatest of the Mysteries), a title given to Dara's translation of the fifty *Upanishads*, was the centrepiece of the whole sequence and the work which had the greatest influence.

Dara's oeuvre[6] marked both the apotheosis and the decline of the great effort to reconcile the two Indian religions, Hinduism and Islam. The dream of reconciling the religious communities ended with Dara's tragic execution at the hands of his fanatical brother Awrangzeb on 10 September 1659, a failure which culminated in the partition of India and Pakistan nearly three hundred years later. After the seventeenth century Indian history was a succession of catastrophes, ending with the incorporation of the subcontinent into the British Empire.[7]

China too was showing signs of exhaustion by the beginning of the seventeenth century. The great periods of Chinese history sprawl across nearly 4,000 years, from the Xia dynasty (2207-1766 BC) to the end of the Manchu Qing dynasty (1644-1911), via — to name just a few examples — the Zhou dynasty from 1121 to 256 BC (which saw the appearance in the seventh and sixth centuries BC of Lao Tze and Confucius) followed by the Han (206 BC-220 AD), Tang (618-907), Song (960-1127), Yuan (1279-1368) and Ming dynasties.

The Tang dynasty — considered the apogee of Chinese culture — was a period of reunification of the empire, which made China a great power in Asia, studded with imperial cities and radiant with culture; a period of reconciliation between the three main Chinese religions (Confucianism, Taoism and Buddhism) as well as a flowering of poetry (Li Po, Tu Fu) and architecture (the colossal Buddha of the grottoes of Langman, finished in 676). All of this is a far cry from the last Chinese dynasty of the Manchu era. But the Qing period was a time of great compilations, encyclopaedias and literary collections. An attempt was made to catalogue what had been accumulated, to measure the present against the models of the past, to get back to the sources by stripping away the layers of supposedly fallacious commentary with which the canonical texts had become encrusted. Poetry, although modelled on that of the Tang and Song periods, had lost its inspiration and become a game for academics, aiming merely to captivate with meticulous pedantry. The period's obvious general yearning for renaissance became stronger as the Western influence began to be felt at the end of the Ming dynasty (with the arrival of Jesuit missionaries): the Chinese had to face the onslaught of entirely new techniques, as well as the accompanying religious doctrines. Even during the Ming period (1368-1644) it had been fashionable to look back to the sources: poetry and prose tried to imitate the great masters of the past, and the poet Li Meng Yang (1472-1529) urged a return to ancient ways, rejecting all post-Han literature. J.P. Dieny writes of this literary renaissance:

> The tendency to revive the past is perceptible in the whole literary output of the Manchu period, as well as its other arts. All the styles, all the schools of the past make their reappearance one by one; but without any feeling that they are simply artificial, sterile imitations: indeed in many areas the Qing writers attain a rare perfection and succeed in expressing themselves in an original manner.[8]

Despite the renaissance in all domains, Chinese thought of this period was not creative in the way that it had been during the Tang dynasty; it was based on returning to the sources and on questioning a cumbersome tradition which, in the hands of some thinkers, had fogged the clarity of the original texts. Hui Dong (1697-1758), for example, asserts that to understand the canonical texts one must go back to the Han exegesis which predates both Buddhism and Taoism; from this comes the name of the Han School (of exegesis).[9] Criticism was used to strip away tradition, to get at the jewels buried in the gangue of false interpretations. But it did not innovate, or launch an era of new insights or altered perceptions. It did not secularize the world or lead to a change of paradigm, the things which were to overturn the modern West. There are similarities between Gu Yanwu and Luther, between the rebellious and libertarian poet Yuan Mei (1716-98) and Voltaire.[10] But despite their originality, these critics did not inaugurate an Age of Criticism like the one which emerged from the European Enlightenment in the eighteenth century. Nor could their work mark an epistemological mutation of the Chinese *Weltanschauung*, since its declared aim was precisely to revive the primitive vision of the past. These critics tend, rather, to demonstrate that the creative momentum of the Chinese spirit — crystallized into cultural canons over thousands of years — had run out, and had not been replaced by a new vision embodying a break with the past. The renaissance, in other words, was not going to lead to the modernity of the new age.[11]

3
The Change of Paradigm

The decline of these Asian civilizations brought their mutual cross-fertilizations to an end. The era of the great translations leading to fruitful encounters between India and China, Iran and India, China and Japan, came to an end. These great civilizations turned away from each other and towards the West. They withdrew from history, entered a phase of expectation, stopped renewing themselves and lived increasingly on their accumulated fat. They were like rich aristocratic families overtaken by events, ruined by a shift in economic reality, who keep up appearances for a time by selling off their inheritance bit by bit: jewellery, paintings, carpets, silver, everything, until the bitter day comes when there is nothing left.

This withdrawal from history can also be discerned to a certain extent in Latin America. Octavio Paz rightly points out that, although the Iranians, Indians and Chinese belonged to non-Western civilizations, the Latin Americans were actually an extension of the West, connected umbilically to Spain and Portugal. Consequently they represent one of the American poles of the West, the other consisting of the United States and Canada.[12] But this connection masks important differences of which Paz enumerates three: the cultural input from civilizations prior to

Columbus via the indigenous communities, the Islamic traces specific to Hispanic civilization, and the counter-Reformation. This last was an attempt to nip modernity in the bud. The Spanish monarchy, confusing its own cause with that of an ideology, 'identified itself with a universal faith and with a unique interpretation of that faith. The Spanish monarch was a hybrid of Theodosius the Great and Abd er-Rahman III, the first Caliph of Cordoba.'[13]

These differences were enough to keep Latin America out of step with North America. For while the North Americans were born at the same time as the modern world, along with the Reformation and the Encyclopaedia, the Latin Americans marched onto the world stage under colours hostile to the modern world, those of the counter-Reformation and neo-scholasticism.[14] Hence, Paz believes, the particular nature of Latin America which is not really of the third world, but is nevertheless very much a poor relation of the West. This has left its mark both on Latin America's literature and on the comportment of its intellectuals. Although Spanish-American literature is modern in the sense that it reflects, in a way, 'the hollow left behind when the old divine certitudes have been eroded by criticism', the same cannot be said of its philosophical and political thought which is openly anti-critical. For Latin America missed the Encyclopaedia and the Critical Age.

> We did not have an eighteenth century. Even with the best will in the world, we cannot compare a Feijoo or a Jovellanos with the likes of Hume, Locke, Diderot, Rousseau and Kant. That is where the great split lies: where the modern age begins, there too begins our separation.[15]

This break with modernity and the social realities embodied in it meant that ideas which could find no counterparts in social reality could only become masks or ideologies. They became screens shutting off the subject and his vision from reality, and this led to a divorce between ideas and attitudes: the ideas may be the very latest thing in political fashion, but the attitudes remain rooted in stubborn atavism.

Thus they display a paradoxical modernity; the ideas are today's; the attitudes yesterday's. Their grandfathers swore by Saint Thomas and they swear by Marx, yet both have seen in reason a weapon in the service of a Truth with a capital T, which it is the mission of intellectuals to defend. They have a polemical and militant idea of culture and of thought: they are crusaders.[16]

The schizophrenic behaviour described by Paz is found in greatly accentuated form in the Islamic world and among third-world intellectuals in general (we shall return to this in detail in Book IV). The moment of separation from the modern world coincides — and this is of fundamental importance — with the change of paradigm in the West.

There, the old world was dissolving as the cultural canons collapsed. Scholasticism splintered into fragments and gave way to the Renaissance, then the classical age, and the beginnings of the scientific and technical era. This turn of events had enormous consequences. It was a revolution both in the scientific domain and in people's way of seeing, a rediscovery of the world, so to speak, through new spectacles. The old paradigm of a world functioning by analogy lost its attraction. Matter acquired new rights; no longer simply the negation of being, it became a creative force of nature. The contemplation of primal visions gave place to observation, then to experiment which could be verified in terms of the laws of nature. Mathematics replaced occult forces. History shouldered its way into intellectual life. In short, there was a radical change which spared no area of existence. But all of this took place out of earshot of the great Asian civilizations, in a cultural zone limited essentially to Western Europe which, from the seventeenth century onwards, was the crucible for the emerging new paradigm and, indisputably, the cradle of modernity.

Parallel with this shift, we observe a re-centring of the economy. Fernand Braudel shows that the centres of gravity move in relation to changes in what he calls the 'world economy' (*Weltwirtschaft*). Each world economy comprises a triple reality: a geographical space, a pole or centre (like London in the past or New York now) and a hierarchy of zones. 'Every time the centre moves, a re-centring takes place, as if an economy could not function without a centre of gravity, a pole.'[17] In effect, Venice became such a centre around 1380, then Antwerp during the 1550s, then the Mediterranean and Genoa between 1590 and 1610. Amsterdam was predominant from the early seventeenth century for nearly two hundred years. London became the centre of the world economy between 1780 and 1815, and in 1929 the centre crossed the Atlantic to settle in New York.

With London as the centre, a page was turned in economic history.

For the first time, the European economy, which greatly outweighed the others, could claim to dominate the world economy and to be identified with it, in a universe where every obstacle evaporated before the English in particular, but before the other Europeans too.[18]

In recent years there has been talk of a new re-centring, this time on the Pacific. The United States and Japan being in a sense the new axis of the third technological revolution, some sort of coalition short-circuiting Europe seems inevitable. John Naisbitt calls this emerging reality *US-Japan Inc.*[19]

What do we mean by paradigm? According to Thomas Kuhn, the paradigm represents the aggregate of beliefs, recognized values and techniques which are common to a given group.[20] The paradigm is a particular vision of the world shared by the members of a community of scientists and thinkers. When it changes as a result of scientific mutations, the world in which the scientists live changes with it, and they see things in another way, as it were with new eyes. A change of paradigm is like a journey from one constellation to another. For not only do things reveal themselves in a new way, but our reactions are different as well. 'What were ducks in the scientist's view before the revolution are rabbits afterwards. The man who first saw the exterior of the box from above later sees its interior from below.'[21] Hence the change of visual perception accompanying every change of paradigm. A scholar newly converted to Copernican theory would not say as he gazed at the moon, 'I used to see a planet, now I see a satellite,' but rather, 'I once took the moon to be a planet, but I was wrong.' Between then and now there has occurred a change of vision representing a refinement of the earlier perception: this corrected vision becomes the axis on which are pivoted both changes to perceived categories and the transformation of psychological behaviour. 'Lavoisier . . . saw oxygen where Priestley had seen dephlogisticated air and where others had seen nothing at all . . . After discovering oxygen Lavoisier worked in a different world.'[22]

While an Aristotelian would have explained the oscillation of a mass suspended from a string as a prevented fall, able to come to rest only after a complicated movement, for Galileo it had become the pendulum: a body theoretically capable of repeating the same movement an infinite number of times. Pendulums governed by the idea of *impetus* 'were brought into existence by something very like a paradigm-influenced Gestalt switch'.[23]

This new paradigm was to find philosophic form in the thought of Descartes where all these elements were already strongly articulated. Here begins the era of conflict between the paradigms, and here begins the age of *non-communication* between converts to the new paradigm, who were going to change the world, and those left on the sidelines who were doomed to suffer the consequences. It may be useful to give a few examples of this dialogue of the deaf. One world corresponds with the other through occult analogy, assert the defenders of the old paradigm. On the contrary, the modernists reply, they are different, they are heterogeneous, there are disjunctions of structure and scale. The world has a purpose, pursue the traditionalists, because cause and purpose coincide in the indeterminacy of being. Not a bit! the modernists answer, it is absurd to talk about purposes where everything flows with infallible inevitability from God as a consequence of His action. But, rejoins the first group, it cannot be denied that tastes and colours are inherent in the nature of things. Wrong again: they are just subjective modes of thought, what we call a thing is just extension having no properties except divisibility, measurability and mobility. But the Images we see in our dreams, our meditations, are they illusions too? Worse than that, they are confused images thrown up by the wanderings of the imagination. So it has gone, this matching of monologues, from Descartes to the present. Cartesian thought is not, however, the last paradigm of modernity; according to Michel Foucault it represents the classical *episteme* (we shall return to this in Book III). This underwent a metamorphosis in the nineteenth century, with the appearance of a mutation of the Historical Order in which the idea of evolution replaced the static one of representation, thus inaugurating the paradigm of the new age.

It was Newton who gave body to the Cartesian dream. Combining the work of predecessors like Copernicus, Kepler, Galileo and Descartes in a powerful synthesis, he became the scientific culmination of the new paradigm. After that, everything stayed in order until the end of the nineteenth century. The world functioned like a machine running in accordance with immutable laws. This model became so powerful, so convincing, that it ended by influencing not just the pure sciences but the human sciences as well. F. Capra, in his book *The Turning Point*,[24] demonstrates the application of the mechanistic concept of life in biology, in the bio-medical model, in psychology and the economic sciences: in other words, all the reductive systems. It should be noted that since the revolutionary scientific developments of the twentieth century

— the theory of relativity, quantum mechanics — there are signs of the emergence of another new paradigm which, compared to its predecessor, has the advantages of being organic, holistic and ecological. But although this new paradigm is more or less apparent in all the sciences, and is accompanied by technological mutations on a planetary scale, the old one is still operational and shows no sign of abdicating.

4
The Struggle between the Paradigms

Thus, the non-Western civilizations are living through a time of two paradigms: their own, and the one which emerged from the great scientific revolutions (what Foucault calls the modern *episteme*). How does a person adapt to a world in which two such different models are facing each other, without running the risk of falling into absurd behaviour? How can he hold back the tide rising all around him? Because, in the final analysis, the collision of two different paradigms lies behind the conflict between modernity and tradition, as well as the pervasive ontological, psychological and aesthetic displacements (see Book III).

On one side there is change, the qualitative jump, progress and mutation; on the other, sociological unwieldiness, traditional inertia, sclerosis and ideologies of combat. Between the two paradigms, apart from differences of all sorts, there is also a sort of inverse historical symmetry. Paz, for example,[25] in a comparison between Buddhism and Christianity, comes to the interesting conclusion that they developed through their various stages in opposite directions. Buddhism, which started as a reaction against brahmanic orthodoxy, very quickly became a philosopy (School of the *Sarvastivadin* of the Lesser Vehicle), then a metaphysics with the great creations of the *Mahayana*, and finally a ritual religion with Tantrism. Christianity developed in the opposite direction: when it first appeared it was a religion of salvation. It created a philosophy with the Fathers of the Church, then became a metaphysics, then with the Reformation (coinciding with the beginning of the change of paradigm in the West) it moved 'from metaphysics to criticism and from ritual to ethics'.[26] The final phase of Christianity is Protestantism, while that of Buddhism is Tantrism. The first represents a shift from incarnation to disincarnation, the second on the contrary a movement from disincarnation to the incarnation of the Images.[27] In other words, in its relations with the body, Christianity has adopted an attitude of 'disjunction', while Buddhism in Tantric form is the doctrine of the 'conjunction' of body and spirit and 'preaches a total experience, both carnal and spiritual, which must be felt and lived concretely in the ritual'.[28]

These differences and many others, of disjunction or conjunction, of spiritual individuation or subjectivism, of abstract or concrete relations with the body, ritual and morality, denote a shift of paradigm and underline the incompatibility of two radically opposed worlds. This displacement was not perceived by the Orientals until the nineteenth century, specifically until the encounter with the industrial power of the West in the age of colonial expansion. Reactions to the challenge were diverse and passed through different phases. Let us take the example of the Islamic world, which is anyway our main concern.

Two periods can be discerned in the Islamic world's awakening to Western hegemony: the 'renaissance' (*Nahda*) and the era of revolutions (*Thawra*). The first stage, according to Arkoun,[29] lasted from the end of the nineteenth century until 1950. The second is still going on and may have found its ultimate expression in the Islamic Republic of Iran. How, then, did the Islamic world face up to this new challenge?

The first thing that struck the Muslims was the reality of their backwardness. From the 1880s onwards a whole plethora of Muslim thinkers concentrated on this subject. It became one of the regular themes of the Arabic journal *Al-Urwa al-Wuthqa* (The Indissoluble Link), founded in Paris in 1884 by an Iranian, Jamal ed-Din Asad Abadi, known as al-Afghani (1839-97), and an Egyptian, Muhammad Abduh (1849-1905). The journal urged Muslims to struggle against obscurantism, fanaticism and social inertia, and to resist Western hegemony in the territories of Islam: hence the ideas of pan-Islamism, of returning to the sources, of Islamic rebirth. The main themes launched by this magazine were carried on by Rashid Rida (1865-1935), an associate of Abduh, in his reformist review *Al-Manar* (Cairo, 1898); by the Syrian Abd al-Rahman al-Kawakibi (1854-1902), and many others. Two tendencies are noticeable in the treatment of these themes: self-criticism (the theme of backwardness), and an effort to promote the idea that the reason why Muslims suffer so many reverses is that they have corrupted the true religion, so that Islam has become 'like a fur coat worn inside out'.[30]

Al-Afghani was the leader of this renewal. In a famous lecture delivered at the Albert Hall in Calcutta on 8 November 1872, he plunged straight into the heart of the subject:

> The Ottoman government and the Khedivate of Egypt set up Schools of Science sixty years ago, but without a hope of achieving anything remotely useful, since philosophy is not taught in them. The absence of philosophic awareness means that it is impossible for them to achieve any results in the other branches of science ... We can affirm that a people that possesses philosophic awareness, even if it is ignorant of specific scientific disciplines, is in a position to acquire knowledge in different scientific domains by virtue of its philosophic spirit.[31]

What al-Afghani meant by philosophic spirit (*ruh al-falsafa*) was the new awareness, the scientific spirit. He was astounded that Islamic thinkers, 'bent over an oil lamp all night long', never thought of wondering 'why this lamp smokes when it is covered'.[32] He was reproaching them, in effect, for their lack of curiosity, their apathy, their benighted indifference. The Westerners had not arrived among us solely by force of arms, but through a whole network of scientific innovations: telegraph lines, railways, steam engines, gramophones, microscopes and telescopes. 'Is it justifiable to ignore all these problems just because they are not mentioned in Avicenna's *Al-Shifa* or the *Hikmat al-Ishraq* of Shihaboddin Sohravardi?'[33]

Other thinkers, such as the Egyptian Abduh, the Syrian al-Kawakibi and the Indian Muhammad Iqbal (1876-1938), explored the themes of backwardness (*ta'akhur*) and inertia (*jumud*), opposing them with the ideas of evolution (*tatawwur*) and progress (*taraqqi*) acquired from the West. The idea of innovation (*bid'a*), condemned by Islam as 'the worst of things', was re-evaluated; there was even talk of reopening the long-closed door of *ijtihad* (individual power of decision).[34] Some even went so far as to justify progress by asserting that the idea was already implicit in the Quran. But apart from a very small number of thinkers with the daring to suggest a brutal break with the past, most reactions stopped short of iconoclasm. Al-Afghani may have agreed with Renan on a large number of essential points,[35] but he was still a militant promoter of pan-Islamism; Iqbal, steeped in Bergson and Nietzsche, resorted to spectacular mental acrobatics in his attempt to reconcile progress with the Quran;[36] Abduh sought exemplary models in the golden age of primitive Islam. It was generally held that Islam is innocent, that it is the Muslims who are corrupt; turn the fur coat right side out and all will be well. During the first phase of the encounter, then, Muslim thinkers remained ambivalent, although they grasped what was at stake. They scented the decrepitude, they saw the decline; but while they wanted progress, most were unwilling to give up the thing holding progress back. In the quest for scapegoats, they displaced the problem onto the institutions embodying the religion, rather than criticizing the underlying paradigm. Islam was sick, they implied, because learning had become the exclusive property of turbaned ignoramuses, spreading discord and obscurantism all around them.

But there was no realization that the new paradigm could be embraced only at the expense of the old one. To assert that Islam is not incompatible with science, that it virtually *contains* science, does not help with the problem of Islam or the problem of science; for the two remain separated by the dead ground of their incompatibility. What it boils down to is demythifying Islam while conferring sacred status on the language of science. Even with the best will in the world, a resurgence of Islam — supposing it to be possible in original form — simply cannot sweep aside the epistemological upheaval which cleared the way for the scientific revolution more than four centuries ago.

The transition from the period of renaissance (*Nahda*) to the period of revolutions (*Thawra*) brought a change of register. Between these periods there are both discontinuity and continuity. The discontinuity involves the modification of language, for this phase was primarily ideological. Arkoun's remarks are relevant here:

It is less a question of grasping objective reality — as scientific thought strives to do — than of transforming conditions of existence which are felt to be unbearable into conditions which are idealized to make them seem more desirable.[37]

In other words, the critical phase of thought — which during the previous period had been especially militant on the subject of cultural inertia — abandoned its epistemological role and became openly sociological. Ready-made solutions were substituted for the earlier fresh curiosity; the newly critical attitude was overlaid with the ideology of combat. But there is continuity as well, for the themes of authenticity (*asala*), of exemplary models based on the first Muslims, of return to the sources, of the miraculous omniscience of the Quran, in short the whole 'mythology' of Islam which had been simmering discreetly in the imaginations of the thinkers of the *Nahda*, acquired a demented quality leading directly — with the help of fundamentalism — to the present explosion of the collective unconscious, in all its terror and misery.

But what happened between these two phases? I believe that the new paradigm *was* internalized, but in perverse and defective form. Let me explain. The thinkers of the *Nahda* may have been ambivalent and strongly attached to Islam, but they did consider essential questions: they compared, took note of the displacement, identified real problems, and above all avoided becoming resentful. The Egyptian writer al-Qasimi, for example, laid into the cultural atavism of Muslims, whose unconditional submission to Allah made them refuse to acknowledge the sovereignty of the laws of nature, of scientific causality. But despite their awareness of the impact of the West, these men were still between two cultures, people privileged to witness the confrontation through fresh eyes.

The ideologues of the *Thawra* by contrast are 'Westernized', having integrated the dominant paradigm — in the form of a sort of truncated modernity — somewhat perversely into their perceptual apparatus. But what modernity is meant here? Certainly not a critical, reflective, questioning modernity but rather the degenerate by-product of a Marxist vulgate, using packages of reductive wisdom to give everything a simplistic explanation. One could say that the new outlook is modern in a way, but it is a *mutilated outlook*. For it remains split from the archaeology of the knowledge that preceded it. It has not emerged (as Foucault would say) in the aftermath of epistemological breaks, but has simply appeared like the last offspring of an amputated line, not even aware of its genealogy. Inevitably, it is blind. Historically, this phase is an interregnum filled with distortions of every sort, epistemological, psychological and aesthetic. In fact, the intersection of the old paradigm and the new results in their mutual distortion: modernity is measured with the yardstick of Tradition, while Tradition is subjected to the violent stresses of modernity. From which there springs another divorce between this mutilated outlook and the psychic attitudes which condition it: since these attitudes have not been adapted progressively to the epistemological mutations of the new age, they remain rooted in the old, empathic vision of things.

And so into the age of two mutually repellent paradigms, one structuring the mutilated perceptions of the outlook, the other conditioning the emotional content of beliefs. Paranoid ravings are taken for authentic discourse; the by-products, the leavings, of an outmoded late nineteenth-century discourse are accepted as a pure, hard Islam. The output of a certain Shari'ati (who died in 1977), a theoretician of the 1979 Islamic revolution, is an illustrious case in point. In many ways Shari'ati is less lucid than al-Afghani. Although the two men are separated by a hundred years, the first emerges victorious from every comparison. Al-Afghani asks burning questions which are still relevant today; Shari'ati has ready-made answers to every question. While the first speaks passionately of the urgent need to assimilate the scientific spirit, the second gives a pathetic display of the most reductionist vision conceivable. He explains everything in Marxist terms of infrastructure and superstructure overlaid with a Manichaean vision of history, via a cascade of chains of identification. Shari'ati's thought is a mixture of two paradigms vomiting one another out. We wrote in another context:

> If we mix a Hegel devoid of the conceptual apparatus of systematic reasoning and intellectual phenomenology, with a Marx stripped of theory and *praxis*, and an Islam cut off from its two poles (*mabda'* — origin — and *ma'ad* — return), we obtain a thick soup all of whose elements seem divested of their ontological tenor, as they have been separated from the base from which they are made and which justifies their existence. Such a thought can only be a thought which has *no purpose*, and therefore *no place*.[38]

This is the state of things that shapes the comportment of the Islamic world's ideological intellectuals, creatures pulled in opposite directions by their political convictions and psychological behaviour. A painful split which makes our ideologues not into critical thinkers, but into crusaders ceaselessly tilting against windmills, to the great detriment of that common sense which, however much it might displease Descartes to hear it, is one of the most unevenly distributed things in the world.

Book III

The Field of Distortions

1
A Consciousness 'Trailing Behind'[1] the Idea

In the long run, of course, the two paradigms can only deform one another mutually: modernity is denatured by Tradition, while Tradition is subjected to the stresses of modernity. Historically, this phase is an interregnum filled with distortions of every sort: epistemological, psychological and aesthetic. Thought is circumscribed by an array of gaps and displacements which are reflected in the configuration of beings and things. The distortions they generate acquire their own sociological foundations; every social class, every socio-professional grouping, every ideological discourse is affected. They are found in the ideas of intellectuals, the psychological comportment of the mob, the delirious ravings of ideologues. Their ravages are to be seen even among the most orthodox representatives of the so-called traditional class, the *ulemas*. Indeed no sector of social, aesthetic or intellectual life is free from these distortions.

The problem is a complex one. I will try to produce an analysis (with the proviso that it will not be an exhaustive one). It is a plausible explanation, but only one among many others. Let us begin with three questions: Where do these distortions come from? How do they operate? And what is their nature?

The first of these questions is ontological: it concerns historical breaks and the change of paradigm. The second question is about epistemology, the grafting and patching operations used to reconcile the different paradigms. The purpose of the third is to study the types of hybrid knowledge which together constitute a world of sub-reality, of *non-lieu*.*

The distortions arise, as we said earlier, from the ontological displacement. The structures of modernity have imposed themselves on all the cultures of the planet, ravaged every domain, and ended by infiltrating our perceptual apparatus. Our way of seeing has become historical, just as our former medieval culture has been supplanted by modern human sciences which are themselves products of the great epistemological swings of the nineteenth century. But this infiltration was not the result of a conscious decision: we acquired the human sciences by osmosis, without internalizing the process which gave birth to them. This missing link has very grave consequences, especially as our awareness has not been modified internally and is therefore 'trailing behind' modernity: so that instead of being illuminated by modernity, our consciousness is clouded by it. What is more, this consciousness is still steeped in the paradigm of the earliest visions, rooted in an experience of being in which the analogical nature of symbols is still operative and the soul bathes in the empathy of social relations: things derived from a mode of being in which the individual, the Ego, gives pride of place to a collective self, the qualities of place and time become extremely fluid and all modes of existence commune in a sort of united co-presence.

All this is reflected on the level of beliefs as well as customs. On the level of beliefs, it constitutes a sort of *meta-reality* which remains distinct from both reality and unreality, a 'meta-reality which is accepted as being the unconscious identity of the community'.[2] An example would be the fundamental concepts of Hinduism such as *moksha* (deliverance), *dharma* (law, order), *karma* (destiny ruling the cycles of transmigration) and *yoga* (the path of liberation), which every Hindu carries within him as an integral part of his being. This meta-reality establishes itself like a sort of dream in the first years of life, and is reinforced by practical experience, by the power of vision, by intuition rather than analysis or scientific knowledge. Indeed modernity, the product of a different historical

---

* *Translator's note:* the French term *non-lieu* used here is a legal expression meaning e.g. no grounds for prosecution, but also has literal overtones implying e.g. non-occurrence, having no place, etc.

context, is brought up short by this almost immutable meta-reality, which is inextricably interwoven with the weighty mass of custom and deep-seated habit. These last represent a social crystallization of this mental space (hence their resistance to all change). Pérez Galdós says of them:

> We see the instant triumph of the true idea over the false in the sphere of thought, and we believe that it is possible for the idea to triumph with equal swiftness over custom. Custom has been made by time, as slowly and patiently as it has made mountains, and only time, working day by day, can destroy it. Mountains are not toppled by bayonet thrusts.[3]

One might perhaps make a Kantian distinction between form and content, assuming that the forms are the new ideas thrown up by epistemological mutations and superimposed on the old ontology of images: they thus alter perception of the world and shape a new outlook before the underlying consciousness (infused with the traditional meta-reality) has had time to adjust. The content of the consciousness becomes, so to speak, the 'raw material' of perception, so that the world represented is modern in terms of discourse but archaic in its content; for between the two yawns the abyss separating a *pre-Galilean* consciousness from a *post-Hegelian* discourse. The result is a mutilated outlook, which reifies the world of the Image and the Tradition while remaining wholly out of touch with the genealogy of the imported ideas.

A consciousness rooted in the subsoil of the collective psyche can only *trail behind* an idea freshly emerged from the metamorphoses of history. This *time-lapse* occurs at the intersection of two orders of knowledge whose modes of deployment are radically opposed. On the one hand there is the culling of myth, the attempt to fold it back into history, an interest in causality and distinctions; on the other, a tendency to verticality, to identification, to substantiation.

> While rational thought distinguishes between image and reality, mythological thought unifies the reality and its image symbolically and through analogy, reifies its own images, attributes physical reality and autonomy to characters and events of its own invention, and installs them in its own space and time, which are and are not the same as ours.[4]

If this consciousness had been formed historically by the crises which preceded modernity, it would have been able to adapt to the changes; but since this is not the case, and the new ideas consequently find no natural point of attachment, they are crudely superimposed on a historically incompatible background which is quite unprepared to receive them, let alone incorporate them. This is the irremediable cause of the yawning gulf which constitutes a sort of open sore in our consciousness. To throw a little light on this particular phenomenon I will cite two theories drawn from very different authors, C. G. Jung and Michel Foucault. The former explains psychologically what the latter only perceives epistemologically, as the product of archaeological mutations. From the viewpoint of the psychic economy, this displacement is a lack of compensation (regression); from the viewpoint of historical discontinuities, it is the caesural division between two heterogeneous mental blocs which deform one another in the course of their unceasing encounters.

Disenchanting the World[5]
Jung writes in explanation of the disenchantment of the world:

> Curiously enough, science began with the discovery of the laws of astronomy, and thus with the retraction of what was, in a sense, the most far-reaching projection. This was the first step out of the animism in which the universe was steeped. One step followed another [. . .] Our modern science has trimmed projections down until they are imperceptible, but our everyday life still pullulates with them.[6]

Then he adds:

> Now that the stars have fallen from the heavens and our noblest symbols have faded, a secret life reigns in the unconscious. That is why today we have psychology and speak of the unconscious. These things would be, and are in fact, superfluous in an age, or a form of civilization, which still possesses such symbols. For they are the spirit from above, and while they exist the mind too is 'above'[. . .]But our own unconscious encloses a spirit akin to nature, liquefied so to speak, whose workings trouble it. And heaven has become a universal, empty space, a beautiful memory of what used to be.[7]

But every withdrawal of projections provokes a compensation, which is the reason why 'whenever an important segment of the consciousness loses value, and disappears as a result, a compensation appears somewhere else in the conscious mind.'[8] In the West there is a substitution corresponding to each withdrawal. The work reduction is made easier by the corrosive effect of criticism. There is a complete negative evaluation of the history of thought whose metamorphoses are found in different forms: passive and active nihilism (Nietzsche), occultation of Being (Heidegger), instrumentalization of reason (Adorno, Horkheimer) or loss of aura (Benjamin). One might say that the common denominator of all these deprecatory views of the mind converges on a central point: the fading away of something that used to be there, but is there no longer. With the age of Enlightenment reason is substituted for revelation; then suffers in its turn the subversion of its authoritarian rule by fundamental drives and impulses.

These substitutions upset the whole system of categories, not just in the domain of knowledge but also in modes of production and social relations. The more so because modernity only saw the light of day thanks to the dissolving work of criticism. Every profound change was followed by a corresponding shift in awareness: between an idea and the consciousness that identifies with it, there must always be adjustment and isomorphism. In the non-Western cultures on the other hand the two phenomena (a fading projection, and a compensation) remain disconnected. For a start, the fading of projections is hardly registered as a historical experience, one lived through internally, but rather as a series of shocks from outside. The replacements that, in a homogeneous society, compensate for the devaluation of a part of the consciousness do not work properly either; because the consciousness, unable to cope with the radically different paradigm confronting it, retreats into the musty but familiar archives of collective memory. Here there is a split between the lost projection and the corresponding substitution, because form and content have not evolved in parallel and isomorphic fashion.

For example, the subjectivity of the Cartesian *cogito* — an ego cut off from its symbols — necessarily corresponds to the objectivity of a geometrical order of reality purged of its substantive forms; in our case by contrast the ego remains very fragile. It suffers from a double deficiency: it is neither the conscious *cogito* behind a subjective discourse, nor the collective ego distilled out of the experience of spiritual individuation (usually represented as an Angel or some other hieratic Figure in the visionary recitations of our philosophers). Our ego is still *underdeveloped*, alienated both from modernity and from Tradition.

This passivity of ego is also a product of the culture and its ethical norms of behaviour. For example, as we are told by the Indian psychologist Sudhir Kakar,[9] the Hindu ideal of wisdom calls not for a strong ego, an autonomous subject supported by an authoritarian super-ego, but rather for a passive ego, based on the memory of a happy infancy, tending to regress towards a fusion with the origins. The symbiotic relationship between an Indian male infant and his mother is a major factor in helping to weaken the ego. Until the age of 5 the child is caressed, spoiled, over-protected, given his mother's full-time attention. When he reaches the age of 5, the mother's role is abruptly reduced and the father takes over:

> In India, differentiation between the child and his mother (and thus between the ego and the id) occurs later and is structurally weaker than in the West, with this consequence: the mental processes characteristic of the symbiosis of early infancy play a relatively more important role in the personality of the Indian adult.[10]

What Kakar says of an Indian childhood is equally true of an Arab or Persian childhood. The predominance of so-called primary mental processes means that empathetic relationships acquire greater importance than the secondary conceptual process expressed through language. Hence our tendency to communicate through caesuras, through pauses and silences; hence too our natural propensity for magical and animist modes of thought. The consequence is that modern ideas from outside have to coexist with an inappropriate content rooted psychically in an earlier age, an age which still speaks the 'animist' language of myths and symbols.

Archaeology of the Historical Time-lapse
It may be useful at this point to refer to the archaeology of the human sciences as explained by Michel Foucault in *The Order of Things*. Foucault's method consists of defining the conceptual background underlying the birth of the human sciences; and discovering:

> on the background of which historical *a priori* and in the climate of which positivity ideas came into being, sciences were established,

experiences were distilled into philosophies and rationalities took shape — perhaps only to unravel again, and disappear almost immediately.[11]

In this way the historical *a priori* of different periods of thought are uncovered, their 'epistemological fields' are defined, their *episteme* — the collection of anonymous, unconscious configurations that made them possible — is revealed. This is the source of the idea not of a history, but an archaeology of the human sciences, something able to highlight the epistemological discontinuities that punctuate the history of Western thought since the Renaissance.

Foucault identifies three main discontinuities: the Renaissance, pre-classical *episteme* which prevailed until the middle of the seventeenth century; the classical *episteme* which came in with the classical age (about the middle of the seventeenth century); and the modern *episteme* which ushered in modernity at the beginning of the nineteenth century. Foucault's research was oriented on the three 'empiricisms', life, work and language — the biological, socio-economic and cultural dimensions of humankind — and he believed that, below the surface, the fields of knowledge are broadly isomorphic.

Now the idea of an 'epistemological base' as the historical *a priori* of knowledge is not new, and Foucault has some illustrious predecessors. In French thought there is Gaston Bachelard in particular, whose theme of the epistemological break or cut-off was fundamental to Foucault and to Althusser. Another important contribution is that of Alexandre Koyré, a French philosopher of Russian origin, who studied the epistemological articulations between different periods of history: for example, the passage from the closed medieval world to the infinite universe of modern times. And there was the influence of the structuralist school. In other words, the idea of a 'philosophic infrastructure' in harmony with the different periods of Western thought was already in the air when Foucault incorporated it into his archaeology of the human sciences. The idea of descriptive representation as the mode of knowledge of the classical *episteme* had already been formulated by Heidegger in his study on 'images of the world'[12] (*Weltbild*), which says that Descartes was the first to make being the objectivity of representation, and truth the accuracy of the representation. This, as the *episteme* of modern times, reposed on five concomitant phenomena: science, technology, art in the sense of aesthetics, culture and the decline of the gods (*Entgötterung*);

parallel events which collectively explained the emergence of the world as Image (*Bild*), that is, as 'a picture of that which exists in its totality'.[13]

Foucault's idea of *episteme* has striking similarities to the notion of *paradigm* developed by the American scientific historian Thomas S. Kuhn in his celebrated book *The Structure of Scientific Revolutions*. I have drawn heavily on Kuhn's paradigm to describe the ontological displacement (see Book II) which separated the West from the other civilizations of the planet at the dawn of the modern age. In my opinion the Kuhnian paradigm explains admirably the change in the scientific outlook of Western man at the birth of modernity. However, Foucault's *epistemes* differ from Kuhn's paradigms in three important respects. First, they do not refer exclusively to science but also cover economics and philology; second, they do not correspond to conscious principles (such as those defined by Newton) but exist below the level of consciousness; and third, they are not exemplary like Kuhn's paradigms, 'which function as concrete models shared by researchers in their scientific practice'.[14] In a word, the *episteme* is more like the 'subsoil' of a system of thought, a 'conceptual matrix' which underlies every type of knowledge in a given period. But at the same time, the two notions are alike in two ways. First, they are incommensurable; *epistemes* differ from one another, and so do paradigms. Second, *epistemes* die like paradigms when there is a sudden change in the cultural landscape.[15] While Foucault tends to consider *epistemes* as being monolithic –– unitary blocks of knowledge whose separating caesuras retain an enigmatic character — , Kuhn sees a change of paradigm as occurring in a period of crisis, in which two paradigms may exist simultaneously and even engage in a fierce struggle for survival. This is an exact analogy with what seems to be happening today in the conflict of paradigms between the West and the third world. In this Darwinian struggle for the survival of the fittest, it seems to me, one has to consider the strong possibility that modernity will come out on top, even if at present there seems to be a movement back to the religious and the sacred. I have used the concept of paradigm in Foucault's sense (of a 'subsoil' of thought), but without the monolithic character attributed by Foucault. Seen from this angle, my interpretation is closer to Kuhn's paradigm.

In the West, then, the archaeology of knowledge is subject to sudden mutations in which one group of concerns is replaced by another, leading to the formation of a new, heterogeneous bloc of knowledge. What sort of *episteme* will prevail in non-Western civilizations which, without having experienced these caesuras for themselves, had to confront the latest metamorphoses of the modern *episteme* during the second half of the nineteenth century?

We can begin by saying that the underpinnings of traditional civilizations bear a close resemblance to what Foucault calls the pre-classical *episteme*. This is based on four similitudes: *convenientia*, *aemultatio*, *analogy* and *sympathy*.[16] This vision constitutes the 'prose of the world', a prose in which words and things are linked in a tissue of resemblances. The similitudes work in different ways; they can function 'from like to like', becoming links in the chain of being (*convenientia*); at a distance, creating resemblances without contact, like reflections in a mirror (*aemultatio*);[17] by *analogy*, which amplifies resemblances through similar relationships, focusing everything on a privileged point saturated in analogy (humankind); and by *sympathy* which runs like a tremor through the whole universe and acts on the depths of things. Sympathy ties the cosmos in with our moods; it is the principle of assimilation, bringing together the most distant things. It draws weights together with heaviness, sucks lightness into the ether, makes things identical to each other, causes their identity to disappear. If its power was not balanced by antipathy, it would have reduced the world to a homogeneous mass of Sameness: suspended 'by sympathy for the pull of a single magnet'.[18]

The *episteme* of resemblance has a distinctive sign: the signature. God has left His signature everywhere in the world. Here, 'signs and similitudes were rolled around one another in an unending spiral'.[19] The world is thus covered with signs which have to be deciphered. 'To know is therefore to interpret', to move from the visible mark to the invisible. Knowledge is a hermeneutics of the arcana, in other words *Divinatio* and *Eruditio* are one and the same hermeneutics.[20]

This *episteme* started to founder in the seventeenth century, when *representation* became the new mode of knowledge in place of the analogy which had served as the pre-modern law of thought. From that point, thought stopped operating in the zone of resemblance. Similitude was no longer a form of knowledge but had become a source of error, of confused mental images. As resemblance lost its credibility, *trompe-l'oeil* came into play: the cosmic illusion, the whole folding theatre. The hero of this new world of mistaken identities was Cervantes' Don Quixote. Cervantes depicted 'the negative of the Renaissance world',[21] a universe in which writing was no longer the prose of the world, similitudes had ceased to be a source of certainty and everything turned to delirium and irony. When the magic is taken out of the world it becomes impossible to decipher symbols, for 'words and things no longer resemble each other'.[22] Don Quixote wanders aimlessly among things; he 'has become alienated in analogy'.[23] Thus *Don Quixote* is the first modern work, for in it, Foucault says, we see 'the cruel reason of identities and differences making endlessly easy sport of signs and similitudes'.[24]

Language in *Don Quixote* is no longer a hermeneutics of the arcane, but has become literature; resemblance, formerly the work of the creative imagination, has become delirium and unreason. The activity of the mind 'will no longer consist of bringing things together [. . .] but of *discriminating*: that is, establishing identities'.[25] The result is that analysis replaces a hierarchy of analogies. Henceforth every similitude will be subject to verification; and, since their number is finite, it will be possible to make a complete list of things, to put them in categories, to discern their differences and similarities. The principal structures of the classical *episteme* are *mathesis*, 'the universal science of measurement and order', and *taxinomia*, which is the principle of classification or tabulation, the best example being Linnaeus' botany. 'The centre of knowledge in the seventeenth and eighteenth centuries is the *table*.'[26] 'This relationship with *Order* is as essential for the classical age as the relationship with *Interpretation* was for the Renaissance.'[27] And just as interpretation was the knowledge of the similitudes welding words and things together in the prose of the world, so the ordering effected by *taxinomia* would constitute the knowledge of identities and differences.

Foucault uses the same term as Heidegger, representation or Representing, for this way of apprehending the world: 'In the classical age nothing is given which is not given to Representation.'[28] Representation distances itself from itself, doubles and reflects itself. Foucault finds its best pictorial illustration in Velázquez's 'Las Meninas' (1656). In it the painter is represented looking at the viewer. The actual models, the king and queen of Spain, are shown indirectly, reflected in a mirror placed at the back of the studio. Foucault sees it as a symbolizing representation: a knowledge in which the subject is held at a distance. The picture also shows what might be called the 'representation of representation', a mode of knowledge in which the focal point on which the representation is pivoted has to remain invisible. Of all the characters in the painting the king and queen are the ones most ignored, but because 'they are wrapped in an essential invisibility, the whole representation is ordered around them; everyone is facing them, looking towards them, and it is to their eyes that the princess in her festive dress is being presented'.[29] The royal couple is the object of the representation but cannot be represented. Setting man at a distance in this way was to disappear with the arrival of the new, modern 'epistemic space' at the beginning of the nineteenth century.

From about 1800 there was a mutation from 'Order to History'.[30] As history supplanted order, and linear evolution replaced spatial representation of the world, man also emerged as an object of knowledge. From the nineteenth century onwards, history imposed its laws on the analysis of production, on the analysis of organized beings and of linguistic groups. In short, 'History' *gave rise* to analogous organizations just as 'Order' had opened the way to *successive* identities and differences.[31] Two phases can be distinguished in this phenomenon which lasted from 1775 to 1825. In the first phase, until 1800, there is no change in the mode of being of the 'empiricities', but in the second phase words, beings and resources acquire a mode of being which is incompatible with the representative world of the classical *episteme*. The philologist Bopp, the biologist Cuvier and the economist Ricardo shattered the forms of the classical *episteme*. Language, life and work were no longer regarded as attributes of one immutable picture, but became specific domains subject to their own historicity. A new dynamism appeared everywhere: in biology, the function gained primacy over the organ, language attacked etymology and the evolution of roots, economics examined the circulation of goods in terms of production processes. In the upheaval of this archaeological mutation 'man appears in the ambiguous position of object of knowledge and knowing subject'.[32]

Man thus emerges from the vacant place he occupied in Velázquez's picture: no longer an excluded king, kept at a distance, but an omnipresent being. He has installed himself at the heart of the world, and henceforth history and anthropology are linked: 'History (labour, production, accumulation, growth of real costs) exists only to the extent that man as a natural being is finished.'[33] While the classical *episteme* did not seek to identify a specifically human domain, the modern *episteme* is overtly anthropological. In it man is both subject and object of knowledge. His finitude constitutes the essence of modernity: 'Our culture reached the point at which we recognized our modernity on the day that finitude was conceived in unending reference to itself.'[34]

The humanism of the Renaissance, the rationalism of the classical age, were certainly concerned with humankind, gave it a privileged place, but never *thought* it. One could say that until the end of the eighteenth century man did not exist, for in classical thought the one for whom the representation exists, who ties together, as it were, the tangled threads of the pictorial representation, is never present in it.[35] It is true that human nature was studied in the eighteenth century, but what was analysed at the time were the modes of representation which made knowledge possible as reminiscence, imagination and memory. Once the modern *episteme* had constituted a way of analysing human finitude, 'it became a question of throwing light on the conditions of knowledge from the empirical contents contained in it'.[36] It matters little whether these contents are located inside or outside man. The central place here is given not to human nature but to man as 'solid reality' and 'sovereign subject of all possible knowledge'.[37] Absent from the classical *episteme*, man has become troublesome in the modern *episteme*, for this new disposition of knowledge ignores the fact that mankind, whose finitude is the pivot of all knowledge, is himself an ephemeral character in the procession of *epistemes*. Man is moreover a contradictory being, a 'strange doubling of empiricism and transcendence'.[38] A role impossible to fulfil, since man can never be free of his doubles and remains, when all is said and done, a perishable being liable to vanish one day 'like a face drawn in the sand at the edge of the sea'.[39]

Epistemological Schizophrenia

What can we learn from this very compressed summary of Michel Foucault's key work? If I have appeared to linger somewhat on the different *epistemes* of the archaeological method, it is because — although some criticize them as too rigid — they throw light on those movements of the subsoil, the caesuras between the different periods of Western thought. This, in my opinion, is a crucial matter for non-Western civilizations, most of which — despite prodigious intellectual achievements — have not experienced these seismic upheavals of thought; have not experienced the classical age, or the critical age, or the modern era. They have instead been subjected to these things by proxy. Modernity was the outcome of an exceptional process, the only one of its kind in the history of humanity. Claude Lévi-Strauss says that Western culture, after stagnating for nearly two and a half millennia (from some time after 1000 BC until the eighteenth century), 'suddenly produced an industrial revolution so wide in scope, so comprehensive and so far-reaching in its consequences that the only previous comparison was the neolithic revolution itself'.[40] A prodigious revolution causing qualitative shifts in the relationship between man and nature, changes which brought about further upheavals in their turn. 'This process, which has so far occurred twice, and only twice, in the history of humanity, may be illustrated by the simile of a chain reaction brought about by catalytic agents.'[41]

Although the neolithic revolution became the property of all humanity aeons ago, the very recent industrial revolution, emerging from the cultural terrain of the West, had not been consciously internalized by other cultures (not sufficiently in any case to reassert their presence in the world). The deep transformation of people's modes of life resulting from this exceptional phenomenon, the mutations it caused in the mind and in our way of apprehending reality, made this lapse by the non-Western civilizations doubly serious.

By the middle of the nineteenth century, when the non-Western civilizations were brought face to face with this unfamiliar Monster, the modern age had already reached the apotheosis of its expansion and passed through most of its epistemological mutations. Order had replaced Analogy and then been unseated in its turn by History. The non-Western civilizations were confronted, all at once, with a whole well-wrapped package of human sciences in which anthropology was sovereign and historicity was seen as the essential human dimension. The only epistemological tools available to help these old civilizations assimilate the new world came from an *episteme* of pre-classical type. They still inhabited a pre-modern, pre-Galilean world in which analogy, sympathy, magical relations between macrocosm and microcosm, occult correspondences between beings and things, hermeneutics, were the dominant principles for understanding existence. In short they still inhabited an enchanted world of projections. It was a dangerous situation, one in which any mistake, any grotesque misunderstanding, any craziness at all, was suddenly possible. Many of these possibilities have inevitably been realized.

The paradigm conflicts opposing the third world to the West have now reached an intermediate stage in which two *epistemes* are intersecting and disfiguring each other. A conflictual, *inter-epistemic* situation has arisen, one which falls outside the monolithic vision outlined by Foucault, who wrote: 'In a given culture at a given moment, there is never more than one *episteme* defining the possible conditions for all knowledge.'[42] Our painful experience demonstrates the contrary: that however variable and incommensurable *epistemes* may be as a result of the discontinuities which separate them, they are not monolithic, mutually exclusive blocs each of which monopolizes a given period; that they can coexist, at the cost of reciprocal deformation. It is thus possible to live through a period of *epistemic delay*[43] during which adherents of an archaic *episteme* confront the forerunners of the world's next conceptual matrix. One example is the seventeenth-century 'debate' between Pascal and Father Christmas on the subject of the void. Pascal's propositions are unswervingly loyal to the guiding principles of the classical *episteme*, analysis and criticism; while Father Christmas, clearly inspired by animistic and analogical views, defends the doctrine of the humours and the four elements.[44]

We also find a particular situation in which two heterogeneous *epistemes* operate in one and the same person, blinding him and paralysing his critical faculties. This is a precise description of the intellectual predicament of large numbers of thinkers in the third world. The 'location' of the *epistemes* is differentiated in these cases. They inhabit areas of perception which are qualitatively different: the psyche accompanied by all its magical panoply of images, and the mind reduced to the ascetic poverty of bare concepts. Describing this epistemological schizophrenia as it affects Latin American intellectuals, Octavio Paz writes: 'the ideas are today's; the attitudes yesterday's. Their grandfathers swore by Saint Thomas and they swear by Marx, yet both have seen in reason a weapon in the service of a Truth with a capital T.'[45]

In this very perceptive remark the Mexican poet and thinker uses two different periods — yesterday and today — to define two different ways of knowing and being in the world, as it were two different historical *epistemes*, one affecting psychic, emotional behaviour and atavistic attitudes, the other shaping the modern ideas which come from outside. Between them lies the *caesural fault*: a split which is especially crippling because it divides the being into two unequal segments which cannot communicate except on the most elementary level, as there is no bridge to facilitate harmonious internal dialogue. This is not to say that they have no contact, however. Indeed it is precisely where they meet that all kinds of distortions arise, as the two *epistemes*, like reflecting screens facing one another, become disfigured by the mutual scrambling of their images. It follows that — unlike the different structures in *epistemes* which remain more or less isomorphic — here there is no isomorphism between form and content, each being drawn from a different *episteme*.

A significant part of the being continues to operate through sympathy and analogy, drawing on the magical reserves of the cultural *meta-reality*; while the other part, drawing inspiration from anthropology and the human sciences, from the social philosophies, from dialectical materialism, is quite capable of mixing eschatology with, for example, positivism. The product of such combinations is always a hybrid which can only be made to fit together by *grafting*.* Using Foucault's examples, we might add that somewhere within us the naturalists Aldrovandi and Buffon and the biologist Cuvier are at odds with one another. Buffon was astounded by Aldrovandi's 'inextricable mixture of precise descriptions, fables quoted uncritically, remarks bearing randomly on anatomy, heraldry, housing, the mythological significance of animals and their uses in medicine or magic'.[46] Why the astonishment? Because their vision, Foucault says, 'is not linked to things by the same system, nor by the same arrangement of the *episteme*. Aldrovandi was given to the minute contemplation of a nature which was already written, from top to bottom'.[47] In other words, he lived in an enchanted world.

Our predicament is that our consciousness still operates on the magical level of symbols, while our ideas have their origins in the epistemic mutations of the new age. Our own world has not yet been wholly disenchanted: the heavens have not been completely purged of symbols, and projections persist there albeit in seriously mutilated form. Despite the ravages which have occurred, our public space still contains faded images from ancestral memory; we have not finalized their eviction, nor reached the point of privatizing belief. Trapped between historicity and the hermeneutics of symbols, we are reduced to every imaginable sort of bricolage.

But Orientals are not the only victims of this situation. Some Westerners embody the same contradictions: I refer to ideologues, converts, adepts of the new bigotry, neophytes of every kind. I have often been taken aback by the peremptory language of some manic Orientalist whose hitherto dormant faith is suddenly illumined overnight by the discovery of a prophetic truth; or by the attitude of some rabid Marxist or

---

* *Translator's note*: the word *placage* used here and elsewhere in the original French text means, literally, *veneering, overlaying* or *superimposition*. I have generally preferred *grafting* or *patching*, sometimes both, as they have overtones of makeshift clumsiness, which the author clearly intends. The word *veneer* has misleading associations in English with elegant decorative finish.

terrorist sunk neck-deep in a swamp of obsolete nineteenth-century jargon. These days one comes across all kinds of converts: German fundamentalists, British Sufis, meticulously conscientious Swiss Muslims, French dabblers in 'a nice class of Islam, rich in cultural appeal'.[48] The most astonishing thing about these new crusaders is the archaic tenor of their language. One would almost think it came directly from the mouth of the Prophet, with its stern imperatives fit to dissolve the thickest carapace of doubt, its sybilline revelations, its rare pearls of truth. Where the discourse of our progressive intellectuals tries to be modern, theirs is pretentiously solemn. We might describe them by turning Octavio Paz's formula inside out: *The ideas are yesterday's, the attitudes those of today. Their forebears swore by the Enlightenment philosophers, but they swear only by the Prophets.*

This then is a case of religious discourse grafted onto an entirely modern psychological base. In any case, most of these converts 'would rather practise Islam in Europe than in the Muslim countries'.[49] Because to live in the Islamic countries, where the devastating wind of fundamentalism blows, would require at the very least a wholesale reconstruction of their psychic comportment, and an equally radical transformation of the habits and customs which have forged the Westerner's psychological structure over several centuries. You can dress up in Oriental clothes, mutter pious phrases in Arabic all day long, yell sanctimonious tirades until you are blue in the face; you can illustrate the most trivial contentions with apt quotations from the Quran, find in it ample supplies of hope, endless reasons for condemning the monstrous materialism of the West and the miserable spiritual narrowness of Christianity. But you would still rather stay at home, snuggled into the warm comfort of some satanic democracy, protected by the rule of law in a 'secular' state, where *habeas corpus* is guaranteed and there is social security for emergencies. Islam and the much-vaunted *Shari'a* are, of course, a most prodigious bounty, provided one can stay in Europe, out of reach of the law of retaliation, safe from the summary power of religious courts, inaccessible to God's mobile patrols, which sometimes feel entitled to seize women passers-by and give them a whipping for the good of their souls; provided one can be as far as possible from that nameless rabble, that faceless cohort beating the air with clenched fists and pouring endless vituperation on all the world's doings. Of course all of this is quite marvellous, as 'spiritual' as can be; so long as it is only the locals who have to pay the price!

As well as exposing the distasteful opportunism of some individuals and the naive muddle-headedness of others, these Western-style disparities reveal the existence of a caesura — I would even go so far as to say *short-circuit* — between different levels of being: between ideas based on nostalgia for a golden age and psychological behaviour patterns rooted in centuries of laicism and secularization. For spirituality — this cannot be repeated too often — is not a matter of conversion, belief or strength of conviction; it is a way of being in the world. It shows in our simplest and least significant actions: the way we walk and eat, our openness to others, our contemplative attitude to time, to power, to fate and silence; in short, in everything which is neither idea nor ideology, and most emphatically not the proselytism of *arrivistes* or the zeal of neophytes.

2
Two Aspects of Grafting: Westernization and Islamization

Grafting is an — often unconscious — operation to bring together two unconnected worlds and integrate them into the coherent whole of a body of knowledge. Grafting attempts to obscure the absence of isomorphism and reconcile epistemologically two different paradigms, old and new, which, owing to the caesuras separating them, have become incommensurable. Grafting consists of making ideas which have no counterpart in reality fit in with the social facts. In a way, grafting reduces all reality to a hollow discourse, either modern or archaic. But this reduction is effected without detailed scrutiny, without proper perspective, without criticism. The graft is a thin veneer covering the unevenness of things: scratch the surface and the faults and defects are revealed. Grafting resembles a gaudy paint job applied to the crazed, weathered surfaces of old edifices gnawed by the ravages of time. Its flashy façade hides a jumble of ruins, the corners of decrepit buildings collapsing into rubble, the ugly scars of unhealed sores; tawdry finery to camouflage muddy rags, ill-assorted hand-me-downs, patched tatters.

Grafting can work in either of two opposed ways, the results being more or less identical. Either a new (modern) discourse can be grafted onto an old content, or an old (traditional) discourse can be grafted onto a new base. In the first case the result may be called Westernization (given the links between modernity and the West) and in the second, which is what most concerns us here, Islamization. The two operations seem to be contradictory, but they are very similar in their outcome: both result in the phenomenon of *distortion*. This is because the 'base' onto which the new or old discourse is grafted is neither one thing nor the other; it is a hybrid, a mixture of the two, and already a zone of diffraction and confusion. In both cases, what is present is a *mutilated outlook* whose vision is altered and twisted as if reflected in a distorting mirror.

It hardly matters whether the graft is religious or secular, the result in either case will be somewhere in between. Either the discourse will be 'ahead' of the base or it will be 'behind' it, but it will never be in step with reality, given that the reality is also mutilated: it does not correspond to the modernists' idea of it, nor to the traditionalists' image of it. Adjustment will be defective in both cases.

Let us recapitulate the various stages leading to distortion. We have already established that we are situated epistemologically on the caesural fault-line between two incompatible worlds — between two heterogeneous paradigms or, to put it another way, at the intersection of two *epistemes* (here I am using paradigm and *episteme* interchangeably) — each of which marks a different 'historical *a priori*'. We have suggested that in this *inter-epistemic* situation the two paradigms meet and, like two reflecting screens face to face, disfigure each other by scrambling their mutual images. We have also affirmed that, at the intersection of the two paradigms, the old one — comprising the content of an awareness trailing behind modernity — becomes the 'raw material' of the new paradigm, so that the world represented has a *post-Hegelian* philosophic infrastructure and a *pre-Galilean* content. Finally, we have seen that at the meeting-point of these two paradigms there arise distortions of all sorts, and that these occur through grafting or superimposition, which has two sides: Westernization and Islamization. But in this battle of the *epistemes*, which is the stronger paradigm, the one that ends by dominating the other structurally? There is absolutely no doubt that the more recent paradigm — modernity in its very broad sense, but heavily contaminated with the magical content of tradition — has the upper hand. Incorporated quietly into our perceptual apparatus by the irresistible weight of the planetary network behind it, it has become, whether we like it or not (indeed we are seldom even aware of it), the *a priori* form of our outlook, the lens that colours our perception of the world. This is the paradigm which is always present, given in advance. And as its integration is not the result of a choice, a natural development or appropriate compensation, but rather of what Jung calls a *regression*, it manifests itself in the form of an *unconscious Westernization*. When we think we are asserting our religious identity and 'Islamizing' the world, we are really practising a sort of *Westernization in reverse*. The new paradigm, diffused through the air we breathe, may be so contaminated with traditional content as to appear unrecognizable; but it is always *there*, even if we believe we have got rid of it for good. Epistemological analysis shows that, in spite of every sort of fogging and scrambling, the 'perfidious' structure of modernity persists and invariably conditions our understanding of the world.

I have written elsewhere, in reference to the contradictory semantic connotations of the terms 'revolution' and 'Islam':

Which of these two terms is the more active, the more determining: Revolution or Islam? Does religion alter revolution by sanctifying and reconsecrating it? Or does revolution historicize religion, make it into a committed religion or, in other words, a political ideology? [. . .] It is not a case of the revolution being Islamized and becoming an eschatology [. . .] but of Islam being ideologized, making an entry into history to fight the infidels, to stand against competing, generally leftist ideologies which are better equipped than Islam, or in any case better adjusted to the spirit of the time. *In so doing, religion falls into the trap set by reason: trying to stand up against the West, it is Westernized; trying to spiritualize the world, it becomes secularized; and, trying to deny history, it gets completely bogged down in it.*[50]

Thus any traditional content, whatever its origins, can be forced into the infrastructural categories of the new paradigm; values which historically predate modernity are reinterpreted through sociological spectacles. Revolution, the relations of production, history, the anthropological contribution of science, combine to form a substantial new framework which is well able to accommodate any traditional content. Within this framework, a content derived from the former vision of things may acquire new resonances, but can never acquire a new meaning. The ideas may seem extraordinary, original, but they remain 'the local vision of a *universal Gestalt*, all the more powerful in that it represents an unconscious form of Westernization'.[51]

Putting the Cart before the Horse

Grafting and patching operations, we were saying, cause errors of perception, mistaken judgements and Manichaean attitudes. They stunt the critical sense, muddle the power of analysis and encourage dubious expedients and facile solutions. Ideas are always betrayed by the facts, because the facts 'trail behind' ideas rooted in *a priori* notions which come from different historical evolutions. For example, Iranian historians studying the passage from the Constitutional movement (1906-11) to the founding of the nation state (1926) conclude, more or less, that the dictatorship of Reza Shah[52] cut short the democracy launched by the Constitutional movement. This assertion is a half-truth. It is based on invalid historical analogies and the associated laws of symmetry. The law of symmetry really applies only to comparable situations, that is, to civilizations which have been through the same historical process and the same epistemological mutations; otherwise the result is a false perspective. Comparing the Iranian case with the classic French example, one can see that it is structurally different. The Qajar[53] sovereign was not equivalent to the absolute monarch of the French *ancien régime*, any more than the still-nascent Persian secular intelligentsia was the counterpart of the philosophic establishment of eighteenth-century France. Behind the French revolution marched a whole procession of encyclopaedists, Diderots, Voltaires and Rousseaus; behind our movement, vague hopes and wishes inspired by the Ottoman renewal embodied in the nineteenth-century *Tanzimat* (reform). In France, the emergence of the new paradigm, and of its sociological constituency the bourgeoisie, preceded the revolution; in our case the new paradigm, having no adequate intellectual representation or structured base in society, was grafted onto a backward, quasi-medieval world inappropriate to the realization of revolutionary ideas. In the context Reza Shah, the founder of modern Iran, can hardly be said to have cut short a liberty which did not really exist in practice (or even in people's minds). He was, on the other hand, trying to give the country the means to develop a secular society in which these notions might have been able to flourish.

This slanted judgement also neglects the fact that criticism of the public and political domain can extend only later to criticism of religion, which requires a preliminary mutation of the way of thinking. Diderot tells us that the Encyclopaedia was created 'in order to change the common manner of thinking'.[54] For the fundamental task is to combat not atheism but idolatry, not unbelief but superstition. Bayle had already opened the way in his famous dictionary: 'I do not know but that one could affirm, that the obstacles to a good Observation spring not so much from the Mind being empty of Science, as from its being filled with prejudices.'[55] Whether the criticism was made in the name of a natural religion (as in Diderot's case), in the name of the tolerance that Voltaire thought to be the very attribute of reason, or whether it represented a dismantling of the confused instincts on which Hume believed dogma to be based, the aim in every case was nothing less than a demystification of what the Englishman Francis Bacon, writing two centuries earlier, had called the *Idolae mentis* (idols of the mind).

In any case, the age of criticism is undoubtedly one of the most fertile periods in the history of thought — perhaps the most determining period — to remain unassimilated by the non-Western civilizations. The main reason for this is that the ideas underlying critical analysis flew in the face of Tradition and broke free from old habits; another is that, with the arrival of criticism, the criterion of truth moves sharply away from revelation and towards clear and rational — in other words critical — thought. In his *Critical History of the Old Testament*, published in 1678, Richard Simon had already set the tone by saying, with Spinoza, that the rules of criticism were independent of religious faith. For modernity was born out of a critique of Christianity (something to which Islam, and the other great religions of the planet, had never been exposed). While religious struggles still occupied centre stage, the humanist critics formed a united front with the politicians; the common adversary was still religion and the ecclesiastical powers incarnating it. In the words of Reinhard Koselleck:

> It is significant that the same person, for example Bodin or Hobbes, was often seen to be both critical of the Bible and 'political'. It was only when the religious struggles declined in importance, during the eighteenth century, that the two camps separated: rational criticism was then directed against the state as well.[56]

But reason had already been separated from revelation by Pierre Bayle, whose monumental *oeuvre* the *Historical and Critical Dictionary* (1695) supplied an immense arsenal on which all the eighteenth-century philosophers drew. 'People turned towards exactness in reasoning, cultivated the mind much more than the memory [. . .] People became more sensitive to meaning and reason than to anything else.'[57] With

Bayle, criticism became the creative activity of reason itself. It was not restricted to the fields of philology, aesthetics and history, but included a rationality which weighed pros and cons, which could be both prosecutor and apologist, and by virtue of this double function place itself above the issues. Its job was to establish the truth. It had only one responsibility: the future. For the truth is never given; it has to be discovered continuously, its errors exposed, its false appearances unmasked, its superstitions purged. Criticism is tied to progress. 'Progress is the *modus vivendi* of criticism, even when — as in the case of Bayle — it has not been recognized as an advancing movement but is seen as destructive and decadent.'[58]

By establishing increasingly subtle distinctions Bayle reached the point of granting a sovereign reason absolute rights over religion:

It is inevitable that any specific dogma, whether it is advanced as being contained in Scripture or proposed in some other way, proves false when set against the clear and distinct notions of natural enlightenment, mainly from the viewpoint of Morality.[59]

As criticism traced this first dividing line between the domains of reason and religion, it was also delineating another threshold that it was to cross only much later: its frontier with the state. This last — I mean criticism of the public domain — was not consummated until the work of secularization had borne full fruit; only then could reason settle comfortably into the reign of criticism. This reign is magisterially summarized by Kant in the words:

Our age is, in especial degree, the age of criticism, and to criticism everything must submit. Religion through its sanctity, and law-giving through its majesty, may seek to exempt themselves from it. But they awaken just suspicion, and cannot claim the sincere respect which reason accords only to that which has been able to sustain the test of free and open examination.[60]

Criticism is now in a position to assault the majesty of power with impunity only because it has already defeated the sanctity of religion. Secularism must come before political criticism, not the other way round. In Europe the ending of the Wars of Religion enabled the monarch to acquire absolute power. By setting himself up as the arbitrator between warring confessions, the sovereign left criticism free to develop undisturbed in the private domain; and the first targets of its thunderbolts were superstition, petrified dogma and fanaticism. It was only after secularizing society and consolidating the social foundations of its power that the bourgeoisie — the legitimate child of the Enlightenment — was able later to invade the public space of politics and start questioning the legitimacy of absolute power.

The intelligentsia of the third world, especially that of Iran (anyway in recent years, for before the war it was more critical), has put the cart before the horse. Instead of separating revelation from modernity, it fastened on religion as a means of liquidating the minimal functional rationality embodied in the old régime. Later, when it found that it was trapped in a theocracy, it was genuinely astonished, and blamed the situation once again on occult powers secretly plotting its destruction. By using any and every means to undermine the foundations of the old régime, the Iranian intelligentsia was also sawing earnestly through its own perch. For the secular opponents of the imperial régime at least inhabited the same cultural constellation as the régime itself, while the distance between theocracy and modernity is astronomical, like the distances between galaxies.

Good and Evil

The false perceptions resulting from all this patching and grafting are expressed morally in the Manichaean view of good and evil. Someone can always be found somewhere to pay for broken crockery. So we need scapegoats: Satans, great and not so great; plots, conspiracies on every side, treacherous cabals seething behind our backs. The good grows here, under this burning sun, the good is what springs spontaneously from this soil: that is what is authentic, that is what is endogenous, and never mind how nasty it may be. The authentic thing may be an idea, an object, a class, an individual. It may be the 'wretched of the earth' facing the 'internal colonist' or (to use more fashionable terms) the deprived confronting the arrogant. It may be a 'cultural identity' — whatever that may be — resisting an alienating modernity; it may be the religion of the ancestors battling the secularism promoted by blasphemers on the payroll of the Prince of Darkness. There is black and there is white; pastel tones, the nuances of chiaroscuro, penumbral shades of grey, the subtle gradation of demi-tints, have no place here. These tenacious habits, this reductionist vision, are so deeply rooted in people's minds that they keep reappearing in different guises. No matter if the premises on which these judgements are based are refuted by the facts; people return to the charge anyway. So that when a sociologist was released from jail in Tehran not long ago, after the failure of all the cultural revolutions, the poor man was still unable to let go and was persisting, albeit somewhat doubtfully, in 'his search for original formulae of development which would not be copied from the Western Marxist model'.[61] How haunted we are by modernity, that 'mirage of development', that aberration which only makes things worse, makes leaders blind, polarizes society, creates 'a Westernized élite'![62] We return again and again to the same obsessions, the same utterly threadbare arguments; but never make the slightest attempt, however inadequate, to analyse modernity itself as a prodigious phenomenon in the history of humanity. As if we could get hold of modernity by one end, fold it up, flatten it out on the bed of Procrustes, trim it ruthlessly down to the limited scale of our own ideas and make a place for it among the phantasms of our so-called 'cultural identity'.

Another author[63] expands equally disapprovingly on the detail of this polarization. Under the old régime in Iran, he tells us, there were two distinct nations: native colons and the marginalized masses. What was going on was a 'mytosis of the collectivity'; worse than that, a *South-Africanization of the country*. Hence the emergence of two antagonistic types of people: the native colon who had his own culture (Western), languages (English, French), schools and mother countries (United States, Europe), and the wretched of the earth who had his. The culture of the wretched of the earth had been discarded by the dominant minority, which had sold itself to the foreigner body and soul and become his servile imitator. More Western than the Westerners, it spoke only foreign languages to the detriment of its mother tongue; some of its members had even surreptitiously converted to Christianity, to distance themselves even further from the wretched of the earth. Doubtless all this is true, but our author stops at the revolution and omits the rest of the story. We are not told what the wretched of the earth were going to do once they had replaced the old native colons. Would they become more evil, more 'authentic', more repressive? We are not told anything about it, and although the article was written several years after the revolution it does not contain a word on the subject, as if it were a matter of small importance.

I have the impression that this language hinges on a couple of basic axes: the dialectic of the colonizer and the colonized and the subjacent, moralizing idea that everything exogenous is necessarily bad and everything endogenous is inevitably good. This leads to a diabolization of the outgroup, and also feeds the larval populism that runs like a furtive shiver through all discourse on questions of identity. The people is always right, because it is a mass hypostatized into a historical *fatum*. Once it has become thoroughly set, this opposition is unable to change, even when subsequent events seem to make change necessary. Most thinkers of this type remain obsessively fixated on an obsolete situation, as if time had come to a halt in 1979. Hearing them, one gets the impression that the years of upheaval reducing the country to a shambles can be treated as a temporary aberration and stuck between parentheses. In the landscape of their thought, the old régime is still the only blameworthy 'interlocutor'. Why? Because it embodies 'evil', foreignness; the new régime by contrast is private, family business.

Another reason for these judgements is a failure to understand the elementary truth that any developing society — any society trying to come to terms with modernity, even in a small way — must inevitably suffer some polarization. The appearance of a class of bureaucrats (a kind of native colon) alienated from popular culture is unavoidable in any industrialization process. It is true that its depersonalized aspect can appear shocking to a traditional society, especially one ruled by an autocratic régime that forbids the smallest participation in politics. But nothing can prevent the rise of a class with direct access to the well-springs of technological rationality. Besides, I cannot help wondering whether there can ever be an intermediate solution between development and underdevelopment. Certainly the excesses of primitive industrialization can have catastrophic side-effects, can provoke violent reactions and regressions; but to cast doubt on any idea of development and try to replace it with some miracle recipe from nowhere seems to me excessively utopian. It is sometimes said that we should adapt before we adopt. All right! But how? Examples do not abound. The Japanese example — and more recently those of Korea, Taiwan and others — shows that in order to adapt you have first to swallow a heavy dose of adoption, enough to make the change irreversible; otherwise a de-railment of the Iranian type is always possible. And how do we avoid all breakage, loss, corruption, trauma and social upheaval, in an immutable world where customs and sociological inertia are so ponderous that they end by engulfing everything, like black holes?

Max Weber has shown that domination is characteristic of every industrial society, and that the destiny of the modern world, like it or not, is to become such a society. In fact, technological rationality is a Western phenomenon which could not have been born in the Chinese, Indian or Islamic Orient. Its emergence is characterized by three elements: first, the progressive conquest of all areas of knowledge by mathematics (the basis of modern science); second, the application of scientific knowledge through associated technologies; and third, the appearance of an impersonal bureaucracy whose role is to fulfil a function unconnected with any personal concern.[64]

The American sociologist Daniel Bell, investigating the structural contradictions inherent in industrial society, identifies three distinct spheres of activity each of which obeys a different axial principle: techno-economic, governmental and cultural.

> These are not congruent with one another and have different rhythms of change; they follow different norms which legitimate different, and even contrasting types of behaviour. It is the discordances between these realms which are responsible for the various contradictions within society.[65]

The main pillar of the techno-economic sphere is functional rationality. It consists (as in Max Weber's theory) of bureaucracy and hierarchy which 'derive from the specialisation and segmentation of functions and the need to coordinate activities'.[66] The criteria of efficiency are utility and productivity; people are reduced to their roles and functions, are depersonalized, so to speak, so that authority belongs not to the individual but to his functional position in the rational accomplishment of tasks. Management, for example, consequently acquires a strongly technocratic character. To this techno-economic sphere, very similar to the one described by Max Weber, Bell adds the governmental sphere, ruled in democratic societies by the idea of equality: equality before the law, equality of civic rights, equality of opportunity, the equality of conditions mentioned by Tocqueville in his celebrated book on America. While the structure of the techno-economic sphere is bureaucratic and hierarchical, that of the governmental sphere is pivoted on representation and participation. In the cultural sphere, like Ernst Cassirer, Bell includes the whole domain of symbolic forms:

> those efforts, in painting, poetry, and fiction, or within the religious

forms of litany, liturgy, and ritual, which seek to explore and express the meanings of human existence in some imaginative form.[67]

The different spheres thus have different rhythms of change. While change is linear in the techno-economic order (where the efficiency principle motivates continuous innovation), in the cultural domain there is a *ricorso*, a continual reversion to essential and philosophic questions. Hence the idea of *disjunction between the spheres*. There are intrinsic contradictions between a broadly bureaucratic and hierarchical techno-economic social structure, a governmental social structure which insists on equality and participation, and a cultural social structure which rejects specialization and emphasizes development of the ego.

> In these contradictions, one perceives many of the latent social conflicts that have been expressed ideologically as alienation, depersonalisation, the attacks on authority, and the like. In these adversary relations, one sees the disjunction of realms.[68]

Since these tensions are visible in Western society, where their progress has been monitored for centuries, it is hardly surprising that the conflicts often become explosive when they take place in cultural zones entirely new to this process. The brutal disjunction between a class of bureaucrats initiated into functional modern rationality and the frustrated masses scattered across the wastelands of history is bound to cause endless trouble. The more so as it is the internal reflection of the same displacement that exists on the international level between developing and industrialized countries, or in the domain of knowledge between the old paradigm and the new. The reason why the 'native colons' have the power is that they also have the modern education and the technical knowledge. Such displacements almost inevitably produce conflicts within the culture, and these are not going to be settled with a few well-chosen moral judgements, or by simply blaming one class (or one world) and absolving the other.

The Sanctification of Ignorance

When these fractures are conjured out of sight behind a smokescreen of anti-colonial discourse, or papered over with seductive fantasies about identity, is not some part of reality being concealed? Are not such flaws the product of 'irreducible disparities' arising from changes of paradigm and sudden transformations of the social landscape? Any technical knowledge — the product of a foreign context, therefore incompatible with the culture of the country — can be perceived as an aggression, an act of colonialism. The essential thing is to know whether it is possible to find an internal substitute for this foreign import. As this seems not to be the case, why go along with the idea that all bureaucrats are necessarily native colons? Is it possible to opt out of the techno-economic sphere, to abandon any idea of trying to develop, to immunize ourselves against modernity as if it were a plague? Why superimpose the Manichaean vision of good and evil on neutral facts devoid of axiological coloration? To do this is to *moralize* something which is not a moral problem. But it is a way of moralizing which inverts values, so that someone who knows (the technocrat) is called a 'native colon' and alleged to be in the pay of imperialism; while someone who does not (the marginalized person, the 'wretched of the earth') becomes the embodiment of good. The technocrat — or anyway his function — is *satanized*, while the ignorant person — or anyway his ignorance — is *sanctified*. The habit of inverting values to associate knowledge with culpability, simply in order to sugar the bitter pill of reality, is extremely pernicious and has heavy consequences. To strive in the other direction we would need objectivity, stoical acceptance of the facts, a patient apprenticeship; even a certain hauteur towards good and evil alike. But alas! Why should we bother, since the guilty have already been tried and sentenced in the High Court of history?

As an example of the urge to pour bile over scapegoats, consider the case of the famous Iranian novelist living in exile in Paris who, no longer sure which star to follow, decided to vent his spleen on the diaspora itself. As a way of getting his own vision of good and evil on record, he made the claim that exiles consist of two types of person: refugees (*avareh*) and émigrés (*mohajer*). Refugees are inhabitants of *barzakh* (limbo or purgatory); by this term — of Theosophical origin — the author means a non-place, exile as interpreted in the popular imagination. By saying someone is in a *barzakh* situation one implies that he is blocked, that he cannot advance or retreat.

The refugee is a sort of wandering vagabond, suffering the same pains of exile as the *émigré* but never able to choose. The *émigré* can choose: he can go north or south, left or right, go to ground here, seek sanctuary there. The *émigré* never lacks hope. The whole universe is his stable; 'he peacefully crops the tender grass of exile'. He has moments of happiness, makes ends meet, cares tenderly for his precious person. He is irrepressibly optimistic even in old age. The *émigré* makes jokes and laughs heartily. He has confidence in his own taste, knows a lot about art and stuffs himself with vitamins to keep his metabolism in tune. He spends time in museums, goes to the cinema, takes long walks in the park, dresses elegantly and wears a tie. The *émigré* enjoys the fleshpots, loves sumptuous parties, is taken in by appearances and lives on dreams.

The refugee knows that his back is broken. He takes shelter where he finds it; he has no choice. Threadbare, banished, an outcast of outcasts, he is perpetually astonished by his own desperate attachment to his bitch of a life. He loves his country, but knows that his own lot is not 'the tranquil breeze of lovers but the eye of the hurricane.' He is without hope. He knows that he will soon start rotting, that his body is already gnawed by gangrene. He is the inexorable witness of his own death.

Both *émigré* and refugee are inhabitants of *barzakh*; but, while the first builds dream-castles, the second with his own eyes gloomily observes his own remorseless decline. His thought is motivated and sharpened by an awareness of his identity. The refugee changes, transforms relentlessly at an accelerating, worrying speed. But the change is not a blossoming of growth; it is a gradual wasting away to inevitable death.

The refugee fears everything: police headquarters, refugee authorities, lunatic asylum. He is startled by his own shadow. He is afraid of losing everything including his pride and self-respect. He takes offence at anything: the grin of a drunken beggar, the knowing look of a fruit-seller. He is afraid his corpse may be a nuisance to people after he is dead.

Thus we are offered two types of man, two types of exile: an authentic one and an inauthentic one. Two existential situations are depicted, with the good-natured, cultivated, 'civilized' man becoming in some way inauthentic, and the crazed, destitute non-conformist, the ignoramus, the shuffling zombie heading stubbornly for homelessness or suicide, presented as authentic. What all this means, surely, is something like: Refugees of the world, unite! Cling to your misery, stay impervious to all influences, you will be all the more authentic for it. At least you will not be *émigrés*, counterfeits, dubious characters taken in by appearances.[69]

Behind the author's moving choice of words lie the outlines of a familiar polarization: but this time the native colons — with a little help from the revolution — have become *émigrés* who are endogenous (to the country of residence), while the wretched of the earth have changed into exogenous vagabonds, a new group of upmarket international tramps shuffling their broken shoes through the depraved centres of capitalism. The confusion, the ignorance, even the misery of the deprived, the have-nots, become values in themselves. Not because they are destitute and unfortunate, but because they are victims and intend to remain so. It is not permitted to improve your living conditions! It is absolutely forbidden to know anything! And beware of the one who *does* know; for to him belongs the kingdom of lies.

When we say that our intellectuals have a mutilated outlook, we are referring to all these mechanisms of blocking and grafting which falsify the representation of things. And when I add that their critical sense is often deficient I am speaking euphemistically, for (to tell the truth) it has never seen the light of day. We are afraid to explore the subsoil of our accumulated atavisms in case we are swallowed up and lose all identity. Suspended in an immemorial past which haunts the labyrinth of our soul, struggling with ideas that rise up like ghosts from nowhere, we now find ourselves committed to the Promethean task of restructuring the world. What choice have we but to resort to patching, grafting, ideological bodging? The tendency is visible in all our products, in literature and art, in the Republic of Ideas. Nobody escapes. Even the *ulemas*, supposed to represent the monarchy of the Divine, are up to their necks in it.

Islamization

Islamization as currently practised is an entirely new kind of phenomenon. In a sense, it represents the ultimate limit achievable by a philosophy of cultural identity when it abandons all restraint and concentrates on blind self-assertion and denial of the other. Islamization also actualizes all the potential distortions lying about in the social imagination (I will come back to this question). Islamization aspires to be a return to the Origin of the Ancestral Tradition, that of the Pious Forerunners (*salaf*): those who lived in the Time Before, anterior to the whole of history (a history which is inevitably one long catalogue of betrayal and deviation). In consequence, it seeks in all things to oppose modernity and the subversive ideas that come with it. After the mullahs took power in Iran, Islamization was applied on a more massive scale than ever seen before in modern history. In a way it, too, is a grafting operation, but an extremely comprehensive one operating in the opposite direction to deliberate Westernization. Islamization attempts to graft the content of a pre-modern *episteme* onto the backcloth of a world which is of more recent historical origin; a world in which modernity has been unconsciously integrated into the perceptual matrix, and therefore conditions at source all perception of reality. This *unconscious Westernization* remains furtively active within the Islamic discourse by filtering it through a mesh of 'historical *a priori*'; and since a certain vulgar Marxism is among the most operative of these, the Islamic discourse is contaminated, willy-nilly, by Marxist categories.

A sort of larval Marxism hangs in the air, clings in the cracks of the religious discourse, gives it a breath of fresh air, 'modernizes' it, renders it politically marketable. The revolution triumphs and the past is thrown into the 'dustbin of History'; imperialism is 'Islamized' and becomes 'global arrogance'; the proletariat loses its status as a class and becomes the ragged mass of the deprived; and finally messianism itself is secularized and changed into historial determinism, bringing the Commissar into curious juxtaposition with the Apocalypse of the Magus.

The *ulemas* were trapped in a new socio-political discourse which quickly became pure *fuite en avant*, since rival groups could only compete through escalation. The new discourse had to be able to fight on several levels — cultural, economic and social — at the same time. On the cultural level, Islamization had to be pushed forward at all costs; this led to the inappropriate and harmful superimposition of Islam — or of forms said to be Islamic — on pre-existing structures from a phase historically 'ahead' of Islam. Hence the gaudy superficiality of Islamization, its hollowness, its swift degeneration into a 'surreal' world verging on madness. The world of the clergy, with its closed system and medieval values, no longer exists outside books, mental hospitals and the walls of holy cities. The country's metaphysical ecology has been profoundly modified: isomorphism between interior and exterior no longer exists. The mullahs' anachronistic world is drifting like a life-raft amid a sea of devastation from which no sector of life, even the most traditional, has been spared. Everything is affected: customs, habits, modes of production, social relations, representations of the world. Historically incompatible worlds lie jumbled together: the latest technology with the most primitive behaviour, cathedrals of thought among ruined factories, abandoned building sites, supermarkets and skyscrapers sprouting like giant fungi. This lurid Technicolor world contaminates everything, knowledge included, and the *ulemas* have become Westernized in spite of themselves. Bizarre concepts, meaningful only in the context of modernity, have appeared in their discourse. Even the most militant discourse shows clear traces of conceptual ancestry going back to the social philosophies, ideas which look like misunderstandings (not to say blasphemous aberrations) when measured against the *ulemas'* own frame of reference. All these deformed ideas create an atmosphere of confused disorder in which Islamic concepts fall out of harmony with each other, like orphans cut off from the bosom of Tradition. It is true that the emotive charge of the discourse often succeeds in masking underlying incongruities, but these are easily enough exposed by rigorous analysis.

One example is the imposition on women of obsolete customs which many (at least those women who have some idea of their rights, of whom there are quite a few) regard as childish. The imagination of these women is inspired more by the feminist models of the last few decades than by the religious ideal embodied in the Prophet's daughter Fatima the Radiant (*Fatemeh-ye Zahra*). Hence the almost visceral attitude of resistance found among educated women, a heroic attitude, astonishing in its courage and extreme tenacity. These women bow provisionally to the demands of the authorities, keep their heads down and their eyes open, and slip back into more comfortable ways at the first sign of relaxation. Even women of the people (of course I do not include those who have become fanaticized), who are more accustomed to wearing the veil, sense that the operation is not strictly religious but a control technique, a coercive instrument to bring rebellious spirits into line. Or — why not? — a perverse way of taking it out on the women when things are going badly at the front or some resounding defeat has occurred on the battlefield.

Another characteristic is a sovereign disdain for what is beautiful. The ruthless extirpation or concealment of any attractive feature liable to stimulate the imagination, the morbid insistence on dark, muddy colours, entomb the variegated charms of life behind a sad, funereal veil. For the present régime, any enthusiasm connected with aesthetic taste oozes with sexually suspect implications. Music, elegance, beauty, anything along those lines, is assumed to mask impropriety, indecency; to represent the seductive face of hidden perversion.

I do not think that this is a specifically Islamic characteristic, although Islam has always disapproved of luxury, and some theologians condemn music and painting. But even so orthodox a thinker as Abu Hamid al-Ghazzali (1058-1111), an Iranian to boot, and supposed to have been severe in his attitude to philosophers,[70] did not forbid singing or music. His *Book of Hearing and Ecstasy* even recommends them. His view was that the ecstasy obtained from listening was equivalent to that experienced by the prophets during revelation.[71] Not only did this theologian not condemn music, but he also asserted that ecstasy is more likely to be produced by poetry than by the Quran. The attitude of another theologian, the strict traditionalist Ibn Taymiyya (1263-1328), is closer to that of the Islamic Republic's leaders: this intransigent theologian thought the Sufis' *sama* an innovation (*bid‘a*) which would produce 'associationism' (*shirk*) and unbelief (*kufr*) leading to drunkenness (*sukr*).[72]

Even so, Islam can hardly be said to justify the total condemnation of these things. But there seems to be something more in the Islamic Republic's current attitude to these matters. In my opinion, the contempt for beauty, the obsessive rejection of everything that might excite the senses, however mildly, expresses a new attitude much closer to the negative ugliness of totalitarian régimes than to the rather stiff bigotry of traditional Islamic communities. This neurotic rejection expresses a ravenous hunger for power, an impetuous desire to neutralize anything that might break the — supposedly Islamic — mould in which the plaster of life is to be cast. And it is precisely this 'modern', totalitarian aspect that turns ugliness into an entire category in its own right, so that it acquires a quasi-ontological status.

Analysing the ugliness of socialist régimes, Cornelius Castoriadis pertinently observes:

It was already known that some human societies had been almost unlimited in their injustice and cruelty. But there were hardly any which had not produced some beautiful things, and none at all which had produced nothing but positive ugliness. We have seen one now, thanks to bureaucratic Russia.[73]

To understand ugliness of this order, one needs to look at the overall nature of the régime; it is inadequate to explain it in terms of oppression, absence of freedom, the planned economy and so on. All through history artists have worked 'to order', in imposed styles, but they have usually had some belief in what they were doing. The empty, cretinous formulism of Russian official 'art' demonstrates simply and irrefutably that 'the artist *does not believe in it himself, and nobody could believe in it'*.[74]

What Castoriadis says about the Soviet régime is also true, in a different way but proportionally speaking, of the present régime in Iran. Like its Soviet opposite number, although in a different cultural register, the régime has flattened out the relief of things under a grey veil of anonymity and reduced existence to the stifling monotony of boredom or the dry gasps of a death-rattle. This phenomenon rather suggests what Milan Kundera calls 'totalitarian *kitsch*': bringing everything into line with *the categorical ideal of existence*. Politically, this could be either the dominant ideology (Islam) or the dictatorship of a single party. Anything which might threaten the omnipresent *kitsch* is banned: individualism as well as beauty, irony as well as scepticism and critical sense.[75] For here everything is on sufferance; life itself is under a suspension order. Any aesthetic, political or human action, any form of rebellion, anything at all that might suggest an alternative to the ubiquitous ugliness, is instantly perceived as a mortal threat, a split, a radical assault on the system itself. The régime erects its very inanity as its *raison d'être*, and gets the sacred and the ugly so inextricably entangled that this confusion itself becomes a massive fraud aimed at suppressing anything that resembles good taste.

Masculinization of the Feminine Archetype. Banned from social life, sexuality has surged back with redoubled force, but in an omnipresent, suffocating, morbidly obsessive form which affects people's minds far more violently than mere lustful temptations of the flesh. Wilhelm Reich condemned this phenomenon of violent rejection in his book *The Mass Psychology of Fascism*, published in Berlin in the early 1930s: 'The suppression of natural sexual gratification leads to various kinds of substitute gratifications . . .'[76] These substitute forms may include militarism, aggressiveness and the cult of death. In present-day Iran the libidinal mechanism resurfaces in other ways. Most of the substitute satisfactions are present: war is sublimated into an eschatological act of deliverance, releasing immense destructive energies in torrents of blood and tears; death becomes the apotheosis of life, and woman acquires the honoured status of Mother of Martyrs, but remains subject to illicit temptations of the flesh which have to be repressed at all costs. The régime's ferocious hostility to the libidinal power of women is the most visible part of this sad situation.

The régime mobilized against women from the beginning, devoting a large part of its energy to the intimidation of this troublesome element which seemed to pose a permanent threat to the new order. The assault was mounted on all fronts concerning women: closure of the Tehran brothels and rehabilitation of the prostitutes by the new Islamic order; revival of fixed-term marriage which, in parallel with normal marriage, legitimizes temporary liaisons with the blessing of religion; the universal imposition of the veil, which caused an immediate outcry; the televised harangues of certain mullahs, overflowing with thinly disguised sexual fantasies; and the formation of mobile morality brigades (*sarollah*) to detect and repress any deviation from the régime's rigid sexual orthodoxy.

A considerable number of women resented being pushed around by the authorities and found oblique, sometimes very astute ways of showing how they felt; but a lot of fanaticized women, on the other hand, assumed a posture of 'masochistic adherence' to the régime. There are astonishing similarities between the comportment of these women and behaviour patterns under the fascist régimes in Germany and Italy. In a study of the ambiguous relations between women and fascism, M.A. Macciocchi points out that:

> fascism sought from the beginning to obtain a form of adherence from women which I will call *masochistic*: the acceptance, in the context of what Freud called a death wish, of every imaginable sort of damage and stress in the name of the immutable rites of the cult of death. Widows celebrated their own *chastity-expiation* among the death's-heads which the fascists chose as an emblem, stencilled everywhere, wore on their berets and embroidered on their black shirts. From this renunciation of life was born *self-negating joy as a positive goal*. It is a joy that goes with woman's relationship with the Power: renunciation, submission and domestic slavery, in return for the abstract, verbose, demagogic love of the Chief, the *Duce*.[77]

All these substitute satisfactions — masochistic adherence, death wish, chastity-expiation, submission to the Power — can be found in present-day Iran in the often hysterical behaviour of fanaticized women. This militant attitude is something new, with all the characteristics of an original phenomenon. What we are witnessing is a transformation of the traditional archetype of woman. It is true that Iranian women had already been emancipated under the old régime; the changes brought about by the rushed and perfunctory modernization of the country had turned them into mass beings, ripe for political conversion; but this last stage was never reached. The final step was eventually taken, very energetically, by the new Islamic order; but at the same time the image of woman was profoundly modified, becoming much harsher than the ideal femininity of traditional Shiite Islam. Let me explain.

The archetype of perfect womanhood, especially in Iranian Islam, is symbolized by the Prophet's daughter Fatima the Radiant. The lineage of Fatima, wife of the first Imam Ali Ibn Abi Talib, the Prophet's cousin and son-in-law, ensures the cycle of Initiation (*alayat*) which began with the completion of the Seal of Prophecy. For this reason she has the title 'Confluence of the Two Enlightenments' (*majma' al-nurayn*). Together with the Prophet, her father, her husband and the eleven descendants she constitutes the Plerome of the Fourteen Most Pure. She is the radiant source of internal truth, symbolizing the self as ideal woman and bearing the image of spiritual individuation. In the ecstatic confessions of the seventeenth-century Iranian philosopher Mir Damad, she appears at the focal point of a sort of *mandala*, surrounded by the Imams.[78] In this mental iconography Fatima, haloed in glory, occupies the very centre of the picture, dominating the field of consciousness. All of this repeats, in a sense, the symbolism of the Centre. For to gain the Centre is to gain access to totality, to individuation.

But with the ideologization of religion and the political conversion of woman, this image of perfect womanhood was eclipsed by a figure perhaps less well-known, but a lot more militant and doubtless more acceptable to the revolutionary fibre of fanaticized women: Zeynab, sister of the Imam Hussein, Prince of Martyrs. Just as the philosopher-mystic of the former path of initiation has become the ideologue of today's revolutionary Islam, so the feminine ego-ideal has become *masculinized* or virilized into the agressiveness of the Zeynab commandos, those female militias whose insatiable zeal is expressed in unceasing calls for vengeance. For the real, historical Zeynab survived the odious massacre of Karbala on the 10th day of Muharram in the year 680 AD, in which the Imam, his companions and the members of his family all perished. Afterwards, she could not rest until she had avenged the blood of her brother. Brought captive to the court of the Umayyad Caliph Yazid (responsible for the massacre), she confronted him with rare boldness, accused him of every crime in the book and called God's vengeance down on his head.[79]

The behaviour of the Zeynab sisters is shockingly harsh and cold. Their collusion in death and vengeance is visible everywhere: in the cult of martyrs (whose symbolic blood squirts from the earth in the famous red fountain in the cemetery of *Behesht-e Zahra*), in their heartbreaking lamentations, in their frenetic slogans of solidarity with the charismatic Chief. Are they not compensating in this way for their frustration, with a transference onto the masculine order led by the Supermale, mystic Husband of all mothers? The image of woman thus oscillates between the two extremes of widow and militant. Praised now as the Mother of Martyrs, a *Mater dolorosa* in permanent mourning (therefore chaste and inaccessible in her suffering), now as an avenging militant, now as a widow available for the comfort of warriors (therefore destined to wear mourning again, since these are the martyrs of the future), woman becomes the perfect symbol of self-negating joy. The war, being a holy one, must continue while *fitna* (sedition, disorder) persists; so women need have no fear that their status will change before the end of time.

A Modernity Driven Underground.   As one would expect, the Islamization of society extends to education. Brainwashing, especially of the young and malleable, is one of the first procedures adopted by all would-be totalitarian régimes. The content of education is modified by the injection of a strong dose of Islamic catechism which, thrust into the existing content of secular teaching, blooms across the surface like oil dropped into a container of water. Just like the other targets for massive Islamization, education remains on the whole an example of patchy, superficial grafting. Most young people — especially in urban circles — are more or less aware of the absurdity of the situation. They know that the present state of things is artificial, contrary to the spirit of the time; that the hurried Arabization, the *surahs* learned by rote, ring hollow and cracked. This produces an ambivalent attitude in the children, who learn double standards (and the double language that goes with them) in the hedge-school of hypocrisy. Their private world is inspired by the heroes of video clips. Michael Jackson, Prince and Madonna are more real to them than martyred Imams; break-dancing is more familiar than the pettifogging ritual of interminable prayer. They may submit to the imperious commands of the religious authorities, but deep inside they are living a secret life in a completely different dimension. This is producing a whole schizophrenic generation even more neurotic than the last one.

Below the surface of clumsily 'Islamic' forms which invade and disguise literally every area of life, the subsoil palpitates with another, more intense life: clandestine, subversive, very much open to the influence of Western cultural models. Under the old régime, militant Islam was the underside of the opposition movement, the refuge of the oppressed; now, after the explosion of our collective unconscious and the ensuing flood of vomit, it is modernity, crouched behind a hollow religious façade, that seethes in the secret underground life of Iranians.

This tendency is so widespread that it has produced a partial rehabilitation of the old régime. Not just among the Westernized classes — who may after all have sold their souls to Satans of various sizes — but among increasing numbers of the deprived who, through the immense domestic upheaval of the last decade, have served as a reservoir of cannon-fodder to gratify the insatiable rancour of the authorities. No doubt martyrdom has its uses; no doubt it is noble, necessary even; but only on condition that it is mentioned once a year, on the anniversary of the Karbala massacre, and not made the alleged reason for every last banal, pointless sacrifice. The Islam that people actually want is one which feeds their imagination and answers their needs, but which also allows them to breathe, to live in peace in a profane environment where the modern viewpoint would also get a hearing. Because whatever people may claim, this is the viewpoint of those representing order, practicality and economic prosperity.

All the characteristic signs of this modern class have made a discreet reappearance in certain circles: people are wearing ties again, using sophisticated technocratic jargon, admitting to the possession of technical knowledge, speaking foreign languages and displaying Western values. The structures and services of the former power have also regained some of their status: uniformed police and gendarmes, army officers, notables, lay judges, even a few clerics who have seen the error of their ways. These days, any person or institution associated with modernity is seen as a source of minimal order and reason, balancing the chaotic magma spewed out by the shapeless organs of Islam in their role of parallel authority with the established structures.

Signs of modernity in dress style or eating habits, in modish personal behaviour — 'cool', the post-moderns would call it — are the new areas for showing opposition. People are turning inward, cultivating their own gardens so to speak: brewing moonshine alcohol, reading unofficial newspapers, watching smuggled videos. They keep up to date on fashion and world events, they are eager to learn, even competitive about it. The veil is subtly modernized, embellished, turned into something chic or even sexy. Foreign languages are to be heard again, and a pointedly solicitous interest is taken in the country's pre-Islamic culture. People are becoming anti-Arab (and also anti-Islamic, the two being closely associated in the collective memory.) Zarathustra, the sage of Iranian antiquity, is starting to supplant the Prophet of Islam in minds heated to incandescence by exacerbated nationalism. In short, people are drawn to anything that looks as if it may help repel this intrusion of archaic forces, this dinosaur from the atavistic swamp of ancient memory (which, one day soon, will evaporate like a bad dream). The phenomenon is as natural as the body's rejection of an unsuitable organ transplant: a primary, almost cellular rejection by all levels of society, underlining the abject failure of the régime's cultural Islamization policy. The general sensibility, the evolving moral climate, new mentalities breaking with the past, are irreversible phenomena not easily restored to their original condition or brought back to the starting line of history.

It will doubtless be said that all these matters concern the educated classes and not the masses. Even if this assertion were entirely true (which it is not) it would still indicate something important: that even if it succeeds in mobilizing instincts and exciting hatred and resentment, Islamization carries little or no intellectual conviction. In the context, this is a pretty severe deficiency.

The cultural fiasco is highly visible in the structures and services and among qualified people; but the economic failures are even more evident, because more palpable and measurable. Economically the régime is still hesitating between two options: to nationalize and subject the means of production to state control, or to build up the private sector through 'privatization'. Different clans — hard-line and moderate, revolutionary and conservative — are fighting it out (although it is not always clear who is actually hard-line and who is moderate). As elsewhere, the issues being debated are well beyond the competence of Islam. For if Islam in the past was never really a political system, still less was it an economic one. The rival factions today simply represent, within Islam, the ideological tendencies which still divide the world: a Marxizing, revolutionary tendency and a liberalizing, conservative tendency. The swing towards a kind of neo-liberalism which is now discernible in most countries (even China) must sooner or later affect Iran, unless the country slides into some thoroughgoing form of Sovietization, which seems almost as likely. In any case, from whatever angle you look at this state of things, it is easy to see that Islam is only a pretext. It serves as a foil to the different configurations of the régime. In spite of its anti-Westernism, the Islamic government welcomes all the West's technological products with open arms, using sophisticated tools, sometimes ineptly, sometimes with diabolical skill. Think of the nakedly exploitative use of the mass media, the casual familiarity with deadly weapons, the show trials and televised confessions organized for adversaries of every kind, Bolshevik and Muslim alike.

The real danger of Islamization lies not in its excesses, its random changes of direction, its blind groping, its utter obsolescence, but in the fact that, being incapable of setting up a structured historical order, it produces chaos; and this favours the more subversive and sinister elements who loiter in the corridors of power waiting for their time to come. Absolutely anything can emerge from this Pandora's box: the most improbable and appalling monsters in the political menagerie, from Gaddafi to Pol Pot via the whole spectrum of crazed visionaries. For the cult of revolution becomes an end in itself, sets up its own demonology. Islam is blundering through adventures which are wholly foreign to its meaning and purpose. It has already injured itself badly, for in trying to rise above history it has become one of history's by-products, just another ideological blind alley.

3
A World which is Nowhere

The different forms of grafting and patching produce an enormous variety of distortions. These can be epistemological, psychological or aesthetic; they also vary according to the proportion of traditional content that adheres to the imported ideas floating in the air. They may, for example, be the result of chains of identification, along such lines as 'Islam equals democracy', 'ritual washing equals hygiene', 'deprived person equals proletarian'. They usually cross historical fault-lines, ignoring the genealogy of the ideas or epistemic mutations which lie behind changes to the socio-cultural landscape.

In the context of the Islamization phenomenon, these distortions may take the form of unconscious (or conscious) reduction of sacral ideas like martyrdom (*shahada*), holy war (*jihad*) or dissimulation (*taqiyya*) to the level of political concepts, so that they come to mean respectively driving force of history, class struggle, law of silence.

The idea of *taqiyya*, for example, has important cultural overtones for Shiites. The commonest meaning is caution or prudence, the concealment of intentions. The concept can be applied on several levels. On the personal level it is an admonition meant to protect the individual against danger; on the religious level, it helps protect the faith against intrusive outsiders; on the metaphysical level it is the meaning of secrecy, the guardianship of the 'sacred Trust' bestowed (amana) by God on humanity. But when this polyvalent concept passes through the ideological distorting field it loses substance, is flattened and impoverished of emotional and symbolic overtones, to become a sort of omertà: the law of silence, of secrecy as it is understood in a clandestine movement, where everyone is supposed to keep his mouth shut.

The idea of martyrdom in Twelver Shiism is inspired by the exemplary model of the Third Imam, Hussein, who died a martyr's death in the month of Muharram 680 while pursuing his struggle in the desert of Karbala. This model touches a particular nerve in the Iranian soul, especially as it has antecedents in pre-Islamic Iran: some people believe the idea may originate with the death of Siyavosh, one of the heroes of Ferdowsi's Book of Kings. Traditionally, Hussein's martyrdom is a rather apolitical cult like the passion of Christ: tears, mourning and passion are the real motives of the drama, not political indoctrination. Most accounts of the event, like the Miftah al-Buka (Key of Tears) and the Tufan al-Buka (Deluge of Tears), emphasize the emotional aspect.[80]

But as it passes into the distorting field, the idea of martyrdom undergoes a first metamorphosis: the idea of blood, of aggression and vengeance, supersedes the ritual shedding of tears. The image of Hussein is profoundly modified in its turn: he becomes a symbol of stubborn rejection, and his unjustly spilled blood the 'motor' of historic change. In modern interpretations (like Najaf-Abadi's Eternal Martyr[81]) attempts are made to re-evaluate the sources; but in the process they are also demystified, desacralized, historicized. The aura which once surrounded Hussein, which made him a mythical personage, is removed. He becomes a much more banal (if more recognizable) character: a hero willing to die for his political ideals. Even his prescience, his prediction of his own tragic fate, is taken away from him. The conclusion is one-dimensional and flatly political: Hussein's act of martyrdom was undertaken solely in order to overthrow the Umayyads. In this way the tragedy of Hussein ceases to be a mythical event situated in illo tempore and becomes an essentially human and historical drama. For the martyrdom of Hussein was originally soteriological: in the same way that Christ was crucified to absolve our sins, so Hussein allowed himself to be killed at Karbala to purify the Muslim community of its sins. Here the distorting field substitutes the linear time of social and historical struggle for the cyclical time of the myth of deliverance. This secularizing tendency reached its apotheosis with Khomeini, who did more than any other Shiite theologian to exploit the memory of Karbala for political purposes. In his book he says:

> It was to prevent the formation of a monarchy and the adoption of hereditary succession that Hussein revolted and became a martyr. It was because he refused to acquiesce to Yazid's succession and acknowledge his royal status that Hussein revolted and called on all the Muslims to rebel.[82]

To return to the subject of distortions, we should add that they are not restricted to the area of conceptual hybridization which we have been examining, but are also to be found in objects, literature and art. For example, they may involve the aesthetic deformation of styles and objects in a traditional environment, like the monstrous changes which appeared in Iranian architecture in the 1950s under the influence of the so-called 'cubist' style. They may appear in the novel, as when some new genre of Western literary innovation is brought into damaging contact with a sensibility which has no genealogical connection with the ideas introduced, but on the contrary is violently antipathetic to them.

All these distortions, however diverse they may appear, have one characteristic in common: *they do not adhere to reality*. Their relationship with it is un-dialectical, ahistoric. They are closed structures which generate their own categories and live on their own fantasies: in a word, a mental domain *sui generis* which confuses time with space, petrifies perception and makes it difficult to maintain any dialectical relationship with the changing flux of real life. The world projected by this distorting field is not a surreal one (although it looks like it), nor is it a hyper-real world of simulation, but rather a world of 'sub-reality' in which reality is conjured out of sight behind tawdry masks, where a lie can become an end in itself and lead an autonomous existence. Here everything is upside down: life becomes death, beauty is ugly, stupidity is a virtue. Take these propositions out of their closed circle and not one of them will stand up against reality. They cannot, in fact, for they have no real content but manage — thanks to an environment of generalized feedback — to live on their own delirium. Indeed these distortions might be termed *second-stage delirium*.

The Aura, the Mirror and the Simulacrum
The reality of the world is related to the way images are represented and
the way things are perceived by human beings. A visionary whose outlook
is transfigured by the world's magic does not see things in the same way as
a visual person living in the disenchanted universe of Gutenberg. The
decline of the image, Walter Benjamin tells us, is equivalent to loss of
aura. When it loses its aura an object loses religious and ritual value, and
acquires exchange value and display value;[83] the singularity of something
unique is replaced by the technical reproducibility of copies. The quality
of perception is a function of the image, and the image is linked to a
support: the mirror, or in other words the world. Relations with the
mirror-image vary with the more or less substantive content of the
perceptual apparatus: the perception may be open to the space behind
the mirror (to the ambiguity of what is unveiled but still remains hidden,
as in the Theophanic vision); it may be limited to a dialectical
confrontation with the mirror-image; or it may overflow its frame and
explode in an orgy of autonomous images, as in the exponential
development of the media. In the first case we would have an Ontology of
Images, each one still haloed in its cosmogonical aura; in the second case
we would have a dialectical relationship with the reflexive awareness; and
in the third case a simulacrum or copy. In terms of levels of reality, we
could say that we would be dealing respectively with a meta-reality, a
dialectical reality and a hyper-reality.

In his book on America, Jean Baudrillard looks at the last two of these
— reflexive reality and hyper-reality — symbolized respectively by the
different outlooks of Europe and America. In doing so he brings to light
something of prime importance: the differing visions of Europeans and
Americans concerning reality, image and simulation. But where does our
own world fit into all this? I refer of course to the 'Oriental' world which
has its own particular position: which is not based on unfolding or
simulation but remains a transcendental world, in which Image has an
Epiphanic quality and appears like the aura of an icon. Baudrillard makes
no reference to this; to tell the truth, it is not his problem. But does this
transfigured world exist at all? If it does, where is it exactly? And if it does
not, what is this world of ours which is neither *meta-real*, nor *real*, nor
hyper-real?

According to Baudrillard, there is an essential difference between
Europeans and Americans: 'They build the real out of ideas. We
transform the real into ideas, or into ideology.'[84] Why? Because:

What is new in America is the clash of the first level (primitive and wild) and the 'third kind' (absolute simulacrum). There is no second level. This is a situation we find hard to grasp, since this is the one we have always privileged: the self-reflexive, self-mirroring level, the level of unhappy consciousness.[85]

America seems somehow to have missed out on the second degree and over-developed the third level. All the descriptions given by Baudrillard seem to suggest it: 'America is a gigantic hologram, in the sense that information concerning the whole is contained in each of the elements.'[86] America is a simulation in which the world only exists through advertising.[87] America is an immense videograph. All these definitions emphasize the same specific faculty of American culture: the power to generate a world of simulacrum in which the image (as in Woody Allen's film *The Purple Rose of Cairo*) bursts, so to speak, through the screen and leads an autonomous existence, creating a hyper-reality. 'It is this fictional character which is so exciting. Now, fiction is not imagination. It is what anticipates imagination by giving it the form of reality.'[88] The American mode of life is fictional because it is 'a transcending of the imaginary in reality'.[89]

Hence there is no support for any reference to anything. The video stage having supplanted the mirror stage,[90] the image no longer refers to anything but itself, so that the simulacrum becomes self-publicity and life becomes cinema, for 'it is the whole space, the whole way of life that are cinematic'.[91] Compared to this mode of pure simulation in which an eighteenth-century utopia seems to be achieved, Europe still lives in a petrified time of uneasy awareness; or, if you like, in the time of the irreconcilable contradictions of the nineteenth century. Its attitude to reality is ambivalent: either it pre-empts reality by imagining it, or it eludes reality by idealizing it.[92] European consciousness cannot go beyond the stage of negativity, and Europeans remain 'nostalgic utopians, agonizing over our ideals, but baulking ultimately at their realization, professing that everything is possible, but never that everything has been achieved'.[93]

Is not surrealism a good example of this same contradiction? What is surrealism but the Faustian soul's ultimate effort to outdo itself at a sublime point of balance 'from which', in André Breton's words, 'life and death, the real and the imaginary, past and future, the communicable and the incommunicable, are no longer perceived as contradictory' (*Second*

Manifesto)? We now know that this dream was never realized, and surrealism remained trapped in an endless oscillation between the tendency to identify with revolutionary utopias and its opposite, the temptation to turn inward and explore the unconscious, madness and hallucination. Thus the whole history of surrealism embodies irreconcilable contradictions: to celebrate madness while remaining lucid, to effect the reconciliation of body and soul while stopping short of uniting them, to attack traditional values while plunging head first into the esotericism of Oriental doctrines.[94] Surrealism represents, as I understand it, what Baudrillard calls the level of unfolding, of the reflexive, of unhappy consciousness.

If Americans manufacture reality out of ideas and manage, for good or ill, to realize their collective folly, and if Europeans transform reality into ideas, what will be the attitude of Orientals to a ceaselessly changing reality which does not belong to them? People from the non-Western world have a passive attitude to these transformations. They not only find it difficult to fabricate reality from ideas, but are incapable of having an adequate representation of modern reality itself. Their problem is not that of hyper-reality or that of uneasy awareness. But nor do they benefit from the ontology of the image which once informed their perception and made the world and its objects appear transfigured, resplendent as precious stones floating before the mirrors of appearance. A world which, in the words of the poet Hafez (1320-90), was still tuned in to the Master of Pre-eternity:

Behind the mirror I was created like a parrot
I repeat what I was ordered to say by the Master of Pre-eternity.

Orientals are cut off from their primary experiences, but have not acquired the reflexive awareness of the modern age or joined in the orgy of self-advertisement in a mediatized world of simulation. So where exactly are they, since they have to be somewhere? Between the meta-reality of a world of which he retains a few shrivelled vestiges, and a dialectical reality whose contradictions have never really altered the content of his awareness, the Oriental remains suspended in limbo, in no man's land. His reality is a sub-reality, both in relation to the aura of the traditional image and in relation to the hyper-real explosion of the media. Deprived of the aureole of icons, excluded from the ephemeral glitter of movie and media stars, he inhabits a world without psychic co-ordinates, a non-place.

A Space in which Objects are Deformed
This *non-place* is historically 'ahead' of the transfigured world of images whose fading outlines still linger in his consciousness; but it is 'behind' the encroaching industrial world, and consequently projects an immensely powerful distorting field within which every object, artisanal as well as industrial, is automatically deformed. While artisanal objects retain a shaky connection with the world which produced them and adapt in bizarre ways to the modernity which caricatures them, industrial objects are quickly disfigured by the dense ambient atmosphere of a Tradition reduced to sub-reality.

For an example of this distortion we need look no further than the Mercedes-Benz taxis in Tehran — of course the same phenomenon is to be found all over the third world. As befits its German origin, the Mercedes motor car has a masculine, virile and functional air. Its shape is rather classical, eschewing the flowing curves and roundness of French and Italian design, and this gives the bodywork an instantly recognizable thoroughbred look. Once it becomes a taxi in Tehran, not only are the features characterizing what might be called its spirit progressively obscured, but the corrosive effect of the distorting field subjects the car itself to the deterioration of the social climate. The sharp, bold lines begin to squirm and melt under successive bangs, dents and more subtle deformations which soon turn the car into something shapeless. Garish, ill-matched colours disfigure it still further, until it looks like a papier-mâché object. Tiny multi-coloured electric bulbs strung here and there around the interior, a collection of postcards (Swiss landscapes, effigies of Imams and so forth) stuck all over the dashboard, a posy of cheap paper flowers smirking sadly above the steering wheel, make a travesty of the interior, overlaying it with the decor of an impoverished rural festival. The vehicle takes on a second life in addition to its intended function. But it is a life which ignores the object's function, organizing the space of a world of which nothing is left but the glaring evidence of its decline, like the debris and broken meats which recall last night's party.

There is another element in this non-functional decorative tinkering. The object is not just being deformed, unmade, reduced to the level of a manipulable toy; it is also, in some sense, being appropriated and tamed. By 'humanizing' it, attaching talismans (like the turquoise-blue amulets Iranians attach indiscriminately to livestock and inanimate objects) to deflect the evil eye, decking it out in magic spells or verses from the Quran to protect it against malign influences, people are bringing the object to life. It is being animated, instilled with a second life, a more substantial and more 'archaic' life which (one might say) springs from the very heart of magic, from a pre-technological animism.

But when detached from its function to become a more malleable substance, integrated with the natural cycles of metamorphosis, the object becomes technically fragile. As a horse on wheels the motor car becomes a mount which, although caparisoned in a richer second life, nevertheless suffers from structural weakness. Lack of proper maintenance soon makes it a 'sick' object: kept going from day to day with the materials to hand, coaxed along, decorated, dressed up like an exuberant bride, but with whining gears and a death-rattle in the bowels of the motor, repaired and patched like an old worn-out sheet, subject to all the tiresome problems of an extremely hard fate. Where I come from, we are resigned about the longevity of machines. 'Didn't she die young (*javanmarg*)!' we exclaim, as if referring to a young person's tragic death in the flower of youth, before maturity. This ritual mourning betrays our failure to come to terms with the thing as a functional object. By denying its functionality we shorten its useful life, but in condemning it to an untimely death we revive it on another level, we turn it into a mysterious object in the image of the humanity it serves: subject to all the vagaries of nature, all the unexpected shocks of a cruel fate, but a magical object, reflecting both the eternal presence of God and the precariousness of all existence here below.

This deforming space which damages the object by pulling it apart is exactly what we mean by the distorting field, with the proviso that it does not affect objects alone but also literature, art, thought and even psychological comportment. Hélé Béji writes on the subject of the patched and crumbling objects that pass for buses in Tunisia: 'When they move, you would not think that they were rolling on their wheels. They slump down on the road as if they wanted to sink into it.'[95] Everything about them is deformed: their tyres are 'ominous illusions of tyres, the curve of a cheek deformed by the lump of an abscess'.[96] The rubber has perished into a sort of whitish material within which there lurks the invisible form of a tyre. The whole machine 'runs obliquely, one wheel in the ditch, humping itself along sideways like a huge war casualty, and comes to rest on its dead tyres with a metallic expiration'.[97] They retain little or nothing of the appearance of a normal bus, like the ones in Germany where they were made. These are vehicles with 'one wheel in the modern world and one wheel somewhere else, almost clapped out, rusted, doomed'.[98]

This fatal 'somewhere else' situates the object in a sort of *non-place* in which it never transcends its condition, never rises above itself, but collapses under its own weight; never fully attains what it is supposed to represent, endlessly pursues its idea of itself, but never catches up. What stands out finally about these distortions is not the bizarre visual excrescences, the bad taste, the excess, the impoverished nature of the representation, the discordant indigence of shattered forms; but the wavering identity of things kept on the margins of reality, only half-finished, only half-functional; half fig and half grape, things which have no sooner come into being than they are old enough to pass away.

The Explosion of the Collective Unconscious
Distortions can also explode, espousing a crazed discourse and occupying the entire public domain, when exceptional events lead to the collapse of an order. Then the half-forgotten, waterlogged vestiges of ancient memory may be stirred to the surface, giving body to all the fantasies of the social imagination.

The old order may have been overthrown by, for example, a revolution. As far as I know the revolution in Iran remains unique among all those which have taken place in the third world. First because, unlike many other so-called revolutions, it was not just a *coup d'état* but a genuine reversal of régime, involving a brutal transposition of values; but also because it was consciously intended to be cultural. Being neither of the right nor the left, it declared itself as concerned with identity, in other words a revolution of the third type. It is true that this 'third way' turned out to be an illusion; that in the event it simply nourished and fertilized radical ideologies which were already in place. But as a cultural earthquake without precedent, it succeeded in bringing about a gigantic explosion of the country's collective unconscious.

To my knowledge very few Westerners — or Orientals for that matter — had the foresight to predict a possible eruption of latent forms from the Oriental collective unconscious. This was especially true in the colonial era, with the exception of Gobineau who brought his own particular intuition to bear on these themes and made very perceptive comments. He saw Asia, or at least the Asia he knew in the second half of the nineteenth century, as a 'stagnant pool',[99] but not a dead one. Because the water was not flowing it was thought to be sterile. Gobineau believed that, on the contrary, stagnant water is 'horribly fecund in monsters and beings which are not beneficial to our species'.[100] What he thought dangerous was the constant interbreeding of 'the most naturally antithetical' theories. Nobody really knew what would come of this 'luxuriant crop of heterodox ideas'. The terms Gobineau uses — 'antithetical', 'heterodox', 'incessant interbreeding' — highlight the incompatibility of the ideas being crossed and the unpredictability of the resultant forms, whose dangers seem to him not so much material as moral:

> Some new combustion of principles, of ideas, of pestilential theories, will occur in this intellectual swamp; and the infection it exhales will spread through contagion, not always promptly, but with absolute certainty.[101]

In other words this unpredictable fertilization results from transplanting an idea into a body or surroundings that are alien to it. In fact, not only are things changed when they pass through the filter of our perception, they become things of a new and original kind. For example, not only does Voltaire's image change when he enters the field of Persian culture — his name changes to Valater,[102] he becomes a sort of ne'er-do-well with his shirt unbuttoned, he spends his time drinking, jeering at mullahs, chasing women and composing satanic verses, but always managing to escape retribution without difficulty — he is metamorphosed into a new character, almost a mutation. In cases like Voltaire's or Napoleon's the transformation is merely amusing; but if it generates totalitarian ideology it can be damaging or even deadly, and cause ravages in the world. Gobineau lived long enough to witness the first upheavals resulting from the Western influence in Asia, like the appearance of schools of innovators in the Zoroastrian and Hindu communities in India and the militant stance taken by Babism, one of the new variants of Shiism in Iran. Gobineau had a deep affection for Iran but, although he admired the Asiatic genius for creating original forms, he remained very much aware of its incoherent and dangerous aspects. Although he could hardly have predicted explosions which were to occur more than a century after his death, he had the sagacity to suspect that something of the sort was possible.

To return to the phantasms of the collective unconscious, these comprise, in the present case, several layers of sediment, whose geological composition was laid bare by the revolution. At the bottom, on the oldest level, are the archaic strata of the social unconscious, drawing on the most tenacious archetypes of the collective memory — things like martyrdom, messianism, prophetic charisma, and so on, all more or less pre-Islamic with their origins lost in the mists of time. These archetypes play in the social unconscious a role analogous to that of the instincts in phylogenesis. Over them are laid the traditional beliefs of the current religion, and the ideas of modernity imported along with the principles of the Enlightenment and nineteenth-century liberalism. This more recent stratum also includes Marxist ideology which, although relatively new, is actively influential because it contains such a high proportion of revolutionary utopianism. While the older and deeper strata transmit the emotional content of their representation to other discourses, the more recent levels are a tangle of reciprocal interference, damage and mutual contamination, brewing a foaming mass of eccentric ideas.

This is the process that projects the distorting field, something which is relatively innocuous — although far from invisible — so long as the socio-political order remains stable. But when the order is overturned these hitherto passive distortions suddenly acquire substance; they are built into new, sometimes utterly crazy structures; they become aggressively invasive, active on all levels — intellectual as well as aesthetic — and give rise to unprecedented forms of social behaviour. One example is the behaviour of the new 'Islamic' technocrat: careworn, scowling, bad-tempered, he never wears a tie, speaks abruptly, never looks anyone in the eye (for he officially denies the existence of all otherness), refuses to read or speak foreign languages and, as a matter of principle, shaves irregularly. Although people fondly suppose that this is 'Islamic' behaviour, it is not really anything of the sort. It is the social product of the resentment generated when a sort of vengeful, militant Islam is internalized by a certain type of blinkered revolutionary bureaucrat. All hint of Oriental grace and elegance, all the elliptical charm which usually punctuates the measured cadences of Eastern life, is ruthlessly purged and replaced with a sort of would-be intractable stiffness. This resonance between two contradictory attitudes, a sort of 'unholy pact', is something new, a *mutant* form which exists neither in traditional society (where, despite all efforts to uproot it, Muslim fatalism — *inshallah*, God willing — is still predominant) nor in Western society where the bureaucrat's impersonal stiffness is often humanized with a veneer of courteous civility.

These intellectual, aesthetic and psychological distortions do not merely pollute the sociological landscape; when they are *actualized* in the dominant ideology, they can scramble whole chunks of reality by giving them new meanings. The scale of this phenomenon can be agreeably illustrated with an anecdote.

It is said that a young man returning to Iran after several years abroad took a taxi home from Tehran airport. On the way he asked the driver to stop at a tobacconist. 'What for, sir?' the man asked.

'What do you think? To buy some cigarettes.'

'If you want cigarettes, the mosque is the place to go.'

'But that's the house of God. People go there to pray.'

'You're wrong there, mister. If you want to pray, you go to the university.'

'So where do people go to get educated?'

'People do most of their studying in jail nowadays, don't they?'

'Jail! I thought that was where they kept criminals.'

'Listen, friend! Got the villains all locked up in the government, haven't they?'

This anecdote depicts a world where all functions are displaced. Religion has become mercantile and baldly utilitarian, the university has changed into a politico-religious forum, prison has become a place of study and the government a hotbed of criminals. In other words, nothing remains in its proper place. The damage is not just latent — here deforming objects, there corrupting a few thoughts or spreading a bit of paranoia — but has been erected into a *total system* covering every area of reality. In a sense, it has been built into the framework of the whole organization of being, a framework based on a gigantic misunderstanding, an immense distortion. Above a certain scale distortion becomes noticeable: people can see it, nothing can gag it or tone down its garish obviousness. The reaction is on a similar grand scale, and most people — at any rate those who are not blind — soon see through the swindle and notice all of a sudden that the emperor is naked. The more practical elements then set about learning to exploit the situation.

Three Types of Distorted Discourse
The radicalization of latent cultural distortions in Iran is a post-revolutionary phenomenon. It is reflected in art, the cultural discourse and philosophy. I will attempt to give a cross-section by arbitrarily choosing three types of discourse on art, personified by three real persons: a painter (a deprived category which only recently emerged from the ghetto), a highly placed dignitary representing the official language, and a

philosopher who is a model of the organic intellectual in Gramsci's sense of the term. For convenience I will call them respectively the Artist,[103] the Dignitary[104] and the Philosopher.[105] I have to admit that these three types of discourse are not an exhaustive sample, but these are living examples which illustrate clearly enough the emergence of a new form of culture, specifically concerned with identity and brutally cut off from the past and from the rest of the world. Here the distortions produced by crossing different paradigms are erected into a global system embodied in the régime's very topography. The former state of things having been set aside, the frontiers between the different domains become blurred. Religion becomes politico-cultural but lays exaggerated claim to the rank of sacred language. For the moment, no argument can stand against these new kinds of triumphalist discourse which, thriving on the ambient psychosis, feel qualified to have the last carping word on every subject under the sun, and to deny out of hand, when necessary, anything that does not fit in with their general line. No methods are thought too robust for making recalcitrants march in step, or hunting them down when this proves difficult; for gagging undesirables, for countering the evil fascination modernism still exercises over certain deluded souls. For was not all this spring-cleaning detonated by the revolution itself? Does this fact not justify any sacrifice? Is not the revolution getting rid of all the disparities which until recently were tearing the country apart, and thus uniting the irreconcilable under a single epistemological law?

After the big clean-up, a new start. The holes are patched up where possible, and much effort is devoted to building reassuring solidity into the new-found identity. This causes a harsh reaction against the recent past. Our three authorities are unanimous on this subject: the old régime was a false and inauthentic order, rotten in its culture, its art and its politics. Our Artist sees it as a shoddy, second-rate order favouring the 'decorative arts' produced by artists eager only to get rich; for the Dignitary it was a decadent Iranian version of Western nihilism; and for the Philosopher, an environment in which 'satanic art' — that is, modern art — was able to prosper. The new Islamic order, by contrast, is meant to be the *antidote* to evil. Above all it is intended to be a workshop for the reconversion of values, a reconversion back to the sources of Islam by setting all subsequent history aside.

What is the nature of this reconverted art? Our Artist's view is that it should move closer to the people, draw inspiration from it, and stimulate and enlighten it in the process. Art should thus be utilitarian, totally committed to the Islamic ideology and pedagogic in content. Any art deviating from this principle is mere noise and tinsel: in a word, 'decorative'. Art must therefore be naturalistic, realistic, showing things as they are, unvarnished, without frills, without affectation. For the Dignitary, authentic art is the product of an artist who sides with the people, who looks at the world from a perspective learned from the people, and who, thus tuned to the wavelength of *vox populi*, becomes the people's guide and advance guard. The Philosopher believes that the changes mean the imminent appearance of a merciful (*rahmani*) art, a sort of new Alliance with the Divinity. It is plain that in the final anaylysis this reconversion has produced another distortion. For behind each discourse there looms the same great illusion: a deep conviction that linear historical time has somehow been transformed into a cyclical time, that things have returned to their starting point, that modernity has been short-circuited.

Our Artist seems to have found this reconversion in utility, in commitment, in the blood of martyrdom and the love of the people. But the themes he evokes in support of his vision bear a curious resemblance to the theory of socialist realism whose principles were declared at the Writers' Congress held in Moscow in 1934. The text says that socialist realism requires art to give:

> a truthful, historically concrete representation of reality in its revolutionary development. It should also contribute to the ideological transformation of the workers and their education in the spirit of socialism.

The *Dictionary of Philosophy* published in Moscow in 1967 goes even further:

> The fundamental ideological and aesthetic principles of socialist realism are the following: devotion to the communist ideology; activity in the service of the people and the spirit of the party; close links with the struggles of the toiling masses; socialist humanism and internationalism; historical optimism; rejection of formalism, subjectivism and naturalistic primitivism.[106]

This is not the place to go into the reasons for their resemblances; suffice it to say that the convergence of these Soviet theories with the ideological function of art in Islamic Iran is truly astonishing. The populist exaltation of plebeian values and the gross radicalization of the function of ideology produce a reductionist logic, imposing usefulness on art and thought, which swiftly and fatally degenerates into a sort of socialist, or rather Islamist, realism. For this reason it seems to me that the popular art of revolutionary Iran is discreetly and unconsciously going through a process one might call *sub-Sovietization*. Nearly all the right elements are present: the evocation of revolutionary reality which replaces the worsening misery of day-to-day reality; the hiatus between two disconnected levels of reality, that of real life and an illusory space which holds out the promise of a distant hope; the pedagogic function of art which is supposed to cure the alienated worker (in this case the deprived Muslim); and finally the crucial role of the sacrosanct ideology.

Our Dignitary is just as direct. He starts by attacking the cultural institutions of modernity, which he regards as being the Iranian version of Western nihilism, symbolized by the Pahlavi dynasty. Everything is included: the School of Fine Arts which when first founded was run by a Frenchman, André Godard; the neo-Achaemenid architecture created in the reign of Reza Shah; the translation into modern Persian of the sacred book of Zoroaster (*Avesta*). Modernism and Iranism are thus tarred with the same brush and both relegated to the junk shop. The only antidote to this sickness is the Imam; he is the only true catalyst, the turntable of reconversion. He it was who swept away the rotten culture of the streets (*farhang-e khiyabani*) and brought back the authentic culture from banishment within the home (*farhang-e khanegi*). The reconversion makes what had sunk to the bottom reappear, welling up to the surface and driving the Foul Beast out of the public domain, restoring the purity of religion, and thus modifying the tenor of our perception of the world and of existence. And what is all this supposed to do for us? Why, to rid us of the malignant Westernization which is the source of all alienation.

The thing is, though, that our Dignitary, perhaps without being aware of it, uses the very language he is supposed to be against: a Westernized language, a *post-Hegelian* discourse able to pronounce glibly on Nietzschean nihilism, alienation, the unfolding of consciousness. He may not have noticed *that the political overthrow of the régime did not change the internalized structure of modernity, but only changed its content*. In other words, thanks to Islamization, he grafts the *episteme* of a pre-modern discourse onto a social reality which is historically posterior to it. Once again we witness the intersection and mutual deformation of two paradigms, with the more recent one (modernity) managing to dominate the other structurally. There is no way around a modernity which, like it or not, has become irreversible, the destiny of the planet and the *a priori* form of our vision of the world.

Everything succumbs to it, starting with those who believe they have evaded it. The return to the self — even supposing it to be possible on a collective level — never reaches the pre-modern Islamic stage. It is not even known where this self is to be found. Those who think they have tracked it down discover that it is already, alas, too late: the self appears under different disguises, decked out in the masks of history. All the instruments used by the Islamic régime — media, weapons, sophisticated equipment, regimentation of the masses — are the infrastructures of a certain ordering of existence which has already incorporated the essence of technology. And this, as Heidegger points out, 'is not just a means: it is a mode of unveiling, that is to say of the truth'.[107] If it constitutes a danger, it is a danger which saves. The wound can only be healed, as Wagner says in *Parsifal*, by the weapon that inflicted it.

Our Philosopher's vision of the return has strong Heideggerian overtones. He sees the fate of the world, of religion and art, through the ontological frame of 'the forgetting of Being'. The art of the West is satanic (*shaytani*) because the truth in it is veiled in the form of the ego, pride and the subconscious (*nafs*). The art of the future, by contrast, the art which is to be born out of this reconversion, is a merciful (*rahmani*) art. The time has come for sympathy, dialogue, direct communication. Here the role of art is obscured by the sunburst of truth, and art sinks back into anonymity. But when religion goes into exile and the Divinity withdraws, then poets in particular begin striving to renew the Alliance (*tajdid-e ahd*), to resuscitate religion, and all artists bend their efforts to completing this sacred task. The renewal is the establishment of the Islamic Republic. And our Philosopher hopes that one day soon there will appear great poets and artists worthy of the new spirituality. He feels that the preliminary signs are already visible; and that the reason why the present régime has lost contact with the arts, has become alienated from them, is that contemporary art is connected with the *nafsani* (satanic) aspect of modernity.

All our Philosopher's sublime reasoning is based on a Heideggerian interpretation of reality. A twentieth-century German philosopher had to devote some attention to the 'historical' stages of Western philosophy, and had to interpret it in terms of Occultation of Being, and had to unveil in his own way the variation of its discourses over time, so that an Iranian, situated as far away from that world as it is possible to be, could read it in French translation and believe himself involved in a problem which had nothing to do with him; and, as an ultimate illusion, imagine that the messianic assertions of a German somehow contain the spiritual truth of Islamic renewal.

So much for the cartography of influence! One wonders what our Philosopher's discourse would have been like if Heidegger had not supplied him with a key to the hermeneutics. What would have been his attitude to the West if the West had not taken a vivisectionist's knife to itself? For these weapons too — we should have the courage to admit it — are given to us by the West. Stuck in the Islamic thinker's scholastic rut, our Philosopher would not only have been unable to situate it — or himself — in any *place*, but would have had even more trouble defending it against the devilish currents of the West. Of all those we have seen so far, our Philosopher's Manichaeism is the most pernicious, because it disguises itself behind edifying words like Unveiling, Truth, Renewal of the Alliance. Grandiloquent terms more reminiscent of the sacred language of prophets than the critical reflections of thinkers.

So it is with Western preconceptions, in the event Heideggerian 'mythology', that our Philosopher sets about Satan himself. And once Satan has been localized and neutralized, the Philosopher angelizes what seems to be Satan's antidote: the new spiritual order. If this order seems indifferent to the arts which existed before its birth, it is because these arts, like the order which supported them, collaborated with Satan and got involved in all kinds of seedy and alienating schemes. In short, they were not 'serious' (*jeddi*) arts; and as they have no dialogue with the Holy Spirit which has taken everything over (our Philosopher included), there is only one thing for them to do: vacate the platform. The situation is not desperate, however, for our Philosopher is trumpeting the imminent birth of a new art. There will come a day which will be the epiphany of a new Alliance (nobody is quite sure when). While awaiting the miraculous appearance of this Great Art, one cannot help noticing that the present art of the country is being subjected to a process of *sub-Sovietization*. Perhaps our Philosopher will point out that Sovietization is a necessary precondition for spiritual renewal and that you have to pass Marx to get to the Prophet. Or better still, that to become the friend of God (*wali*) you must first have been the friend of the people.

Looking at the multiple distortions we have been describing throughout this book, one cannot help noticing that apart from their hybrid composition they are all more or less inspired by a reductionist logic. Satanization of the other is glorification of the self; native colons versus wretched of the earth, refugees versus émigrés, street culture versus authentic culture, merciful art versus satanic art. Everything comes down to an irreducible opposition, which can only function through a crazed eulogy of the self and a demented rejection of the other. And it can only operate with the aid of grafting and patching, because part of our being remains fatally, irremediably, unconsciously Western. What is rejected is not the West as we have discovered it, but the West as it has deconstructed itself. The West in our time is being subjected to the full force of the boomerang effect of its own exported ideas. The other's look mirroring your own: all that the West had thrust away is rolling irresistibly back over it, enriched with the compost of a thousand misunderstandings; all that it thought it had banished is surging up again, swollen with the amplifying effect of a thousand magnifying glasses.

Thus, we have discovered the West with the aid of its own philosophers, psychologists and sociologists. Our perception is *mutilated*: critical of the West but blind where we ourselves are concerned. It is true that we are validated by criticism of the other, that we become ourselves only through negation of the other. But we have not yet managed the next stage which would involve denying this negation (the negation of the négation, Hegel would say) and discovering that the other is different from the self, but identical at the same time. This will require another level of consciousness. Perhaps — who knows? — another level of objectification, with the paradoxical side-effect of an internal impoverishment of the being.

Book IV

The Social Foundations
of the Distortions

1
Intellectuals

Let us begin by saying that a large part of the Muslim world's intelligentsia is affected by the distorting field. We should also note that the functions of intellectual, scientist, manager, are less distinct from one another than they are in the West. For the great mass of our co-religionists, an intellectual is probably anyone who knows how to read and write, anyone who works with his mind, whether he be doctor, writer, translator, engineer, teacher or manager. The intellectual as society's 'unhappy consciousness', as a member of a separate group whose epistemological function is criticism, does not yet exist in our countries. That is why he does not really have a specific status. The most admired intellectuals at present are those who oppose the régime and whose activities are meant to be primarily political. These constitute, so to speak, the hard core of committed intellectuals, and are really closer to being ideologues.

Of the various jobs which fall to our intellectuals, one of the most important must be translation, which has an essential role particularly in countries which were never colonized and which therefore never used a foreign language as a vehicle for culture. Because they have access to modern sources of knowledge, translators enjoy almost the same prestige as the thinkers whose work they interpret. They are the intermediaries of knowledge, the people who adapt the products of the human and natural sciences to an environment which is wholly alien, not to say hostile, to these ideas. In published works the name of the translator is given a prominence at least as great as that of the author.

Next comes the bulk of essayists, writers and journalists whose knowledge of language is limited (of course there are many exceptions) and who therefore depend on these translations, most of which are extremely bad. Since many of them have been made by people with insufficient grasp of the material they contain, they have nourished a whole generation of writers and intellectuals who, rummaging here and there for disconnected, unravelled snippets of information, use the results in eccentric ways to prop up their own ideas. Hence the sweeping judgements, hence the reductionist visions based on anathema rather than solid, critical reasoning. Apart from this, as the translations are made without a coherent policy, without an overview, they do not appear as harmonious blocs of knowledge more or less representative of some school of thought, but as scattered fragments of learning in no particular context; so that instead of orienting the reader in a specific area, they lose him in the labyrinth of the human sciences. A philosophical atlas, locating the areas and currents of thought in an appropriate overall framework, is sorely lacking.

It is usual to read a book by Sartre, for example, without knowing anything about his role in contemporary French thought, the sources on which he draws, the family of ideas to which he is linked, his connections with German existentialism or his place in contemporary European philosophy. Freud is seen as the promoter of sexuality and therefore 'obscene' (and the target of unbelievable enormities from the pens of Islamic ideologues), but people are quite unaware of the epistemological breaks his thought opened in the mainstream of modern rationalism, and make very little of the vast scope of his psychology of the deep unconscious. Different historical periods are telescoped together with innocent brutality, and the breaks between one period and another are seldom made apparent. Because he lacks a linear conception of history, the reader does not know which are the conceptual structures underlying this or that period of Western history (which has become, willy-nilly, the history of the entire planet).

These yawning lacunae make it impossible to fashion a coherent body of learning. Because they resemble 'holes' in the fabric of knowledge, they are often bridged or filled in by impatient readers with hasty approximations or wholly fantastic conclusions, leading these hapless thinkers into the most extravagant views imaginable. The terminological distortions — already numerous — are then joined by hallucinatory deformations straight out of the imagination. The mistakes and misunderstandings accumulate, grow and multiply, breeding in their turn others even more grotesque, until we are left in a world of distorting mirrors where all the essential ideas are vitiated at the outset. These false assimilations create a false awareness which the critical sense — whose job is to deconstruct ideas and attach them to their correct contexts — is too weak to improve. What is more, the (often unconscious) religious charge present in the thought gives it a bias towards mythologization, while the analytic spirit, which seeks to break things down into their simple components, has not taken root. So the syncretistic tendency predominates, welds the most heterogeneous ideas randomly together and projects a zone of conceptual hybridization.

Another reason for the importance of translations is the fact that we have done very little thinking on our own behalf. Our culture, which is rich but medieval in structure, hardly enables us to understand the great caesuras of the modern age, let alone turn them to account. We have been 'out of step', effectively unable to make sense of the great transformations affecting the rest of the world, for several centuries. These displacements have made us even more dependent on Western science. The dependency is more cultural than economic or political.

Through their role in forging a vague, imprecise terminology, bad translations have become the active agents of an immense field of conceptual distortions. There are several reasons. Although most translators have a reasonably thorough knowledge of their own mother tongue, their knowledge of foreign languages, often acquired with great effort at an advanced age, leaves a lot to be desired. Even where this is not a problem, there are still two major hurdles for the translator: one relates to the heritage of Western culture, the other to the scholastic science of the world of Iranian Islam. A translator with adequate ability in both languages, who is also soundly initiated into both cultures, is a very rare bird indeed.

Furthermore, the choice of subjects for translation is not made by affinity, through a wish to extend the tree of knowledge or mark out known territory, but through ideological inclination. One result of this ideological tendency is that, thanks to the efforts of the Tudeh Party during the 1940s, a large part of the *oeuvre* of Maxim Gorki was translated into Persian, so that Gorki is now recognized in Iran as the most progressive writer of the modern age; through a similar process involving the same universal homage, Romain Rolland has become the world's greatest writer.

A further complication is the problem of translations of translations: an English work will be translated into Persian from its French version, or a German one from its English translation. Translations into Persian of works which have already lost something in translation multiply the scope for misunderstandings and strengthen the distorting field of ideas.

Sometimes an author who is little known or regarded as mediocre in Europe acquires, through a happy accident of translation, an importance which is not justified by his reputation (or indeed his profundity). Gustave Le Bon's *La Civilisation des Arabes* has been treated as an infallible work of reference by several generations of Iranian mullahs. Le Bon, a firm believer in the greatness of the Arabs, gave these reasons for their decadence: the decline of their bellicose instinct, the burden of an unchanging law which prevented progress, and racial mixing.[1]

Most Iranian Islamic thinkers owe their entire knowledge of Hegel to Hamid Enayat's Persian translation of a book by W.T. Stace.[2] The translation is certainly excellent, but is not an adequate basis for any solid conclusions on that giant of German thought. A large part of the comparative work of Morteza Motahhari, a theologian and philosopher of high renown,[3] is inspired by this translation. In fact, Motahhari often gets Stace and Hegel confused, and the quotations given in some of his essays are Stace's words, not Hegel's.[4] But even more shocking than this confusion is the scrambling of contexts. Motahhari and Hegel do not speak the same language and do not refer to the same metaphysical background. It is through a pre-Galilean conceptual screen and with an unshakeable conviction of Islamic superiority that Motahhari expects to comprehend the Hegelian world, and the post-Hegelian one too since he lived in the second half of the twentieth century. If he was just trying to understand Hegel this attitude might still be legitimate; but Motahhari also tries to criticize a thinker whose language and world are totally foreign to him, cut off by the epistemological fissures resulting from changes of paradigm and world vision. Even if Motahhari had been a virtuoso of brilliant perspicacity, the Persian translation of an English work on Hegel would never have enabled him to grasp the genealogical connotations of the German thinker's mind. For example, Motahhari is astonished beyond all measure by the distinction Hegel establishes between Cause and Reason. The distinction is crucial since it is the very foundation of the system of Reason, which presupposes a prime principle which is not a Cause, of which the world would be the effect, but a Reason, of which the universe is the logical consequence.

Motahhari, supported by the presumption of the primacy of being in Islamic gnosis, blithely asserts that the distinction is invalid, since in this case the prime cause is self-creating, free from all other cause, self-revealed, independent of all reason, and the explanatory cause and reason for the whole universe. So much for the distinction. But our two thinkers are not on the same wavelength, indeed far from it. One speaks the language of philosophy, the other sinks into the speculations of high theosophy. Somewhere between the two — a fact which seems to have escaped Motahhari — the primacy has been shifted from being to knowing; also between them is old Descartes, of whom Hegel said, not without admiration, that he had found the new soil of philosophy: subjectivity.

It is also worth noting that there are quite large numbers of intellectuals who know Western thought well but are not capable of translating it into their mother tongue. These are people who, after studying abroad since childhood or adolescence, have lost contact with their home countries. A few do manage to restore the situation, make the effort to compensate for lost time and reach a more or less adequate means of expression. But they are rare, because to do this takes a willingness to go back and learn, a painful apprenticeship and endless patience. It also involves a remodelling of habits of thought, something which does not always come easily. In general, while a few young people trained in the disciplines of the modern human sciences rediscover their own culture through the deforming prism of tendentious Orientalists, others who have not left the country do the same thing in reverse: learn about the West through bad translations by 'indigenous' Occidentalists. Both Occidentalists and so-called traditionalists are in a dilemma. There is always something wrong somewhere, a missing link, some lacuna that needs to be filled; wherever one looks there are these unsightly holes in the tissue of knowledge.

Multiple Levels of Cleavage

Important cleavages can be discerned inside the country, differences caused by the current standing of the social classes and the popular or modern cultures associated with them. While the prosperous Westernized classes stay more or less on the fringes of the country's intellectual life, the same does not apply to the urban petty bourgeoisie which forms the mass of educated people and intellectuals, people who decipher foreign books with difficulty and usually depend on translations.[5] It is these — often very politicized — individuals who constitute, as it were by right, the nucleus of intellectuals which sets the country's standards: they write articles in newspapers, periodicals and reviews, give lectures and seminars all over the place. From their unassailable ramparts they impose a dictatorship of bad taste and mediocrity. Owing to its middle-class origins, this group is emotionally attuned to the culture of the people while also enjoying a certain level of traditional education. It is true that this early, family-based acculturation is often deformed by higher education, but such individuals are equally ill at ease in the company of the richer and more Westernized class of technocrats.

What is understood by the term petty bourgeoisie? The explanation sketched by A. Laroui seems plausible.[6] In Marxist analysis, Laroui tells us, the petty bourgeoisie is not a class. What is more, Marxism is based on the negation of the petty bourgeoisie as such. Compared to the classic triad of landed aristocracy, bourgeoisie and proletariat, it is a ramshackle patchwork of a class; a heterogeneous collection of groups and sub-groups which has no rationally defined place in the system, and is therefore inclined to withdraw into a nostalgic past. In Iran it forms a diverse and very extensive middle class embracing small bazaar traders, certain categories of civil servant, small landowners and so on. Culturally it is much more attached to traditional values than the better-off strata of officials, industrialists and businessmen.

In Islamic countries the three main classes are numerically small. In Iran, for example, the landed aristocracy was broken by the agrarian reform launched by Mohammad Reza Shah Pahlavi (1919-80) during the 1960s. The proletariat generated by the new industries is not very large, and thanks to the sovereign's 'white revolution' is also a relatively comfortable class (legally entitled to a share of profits). The industrial bourgeoisie is a new phenomenon which has appeared during the massive industrialization of the country over the past twenty years. Laroui is right when he says that in Islamic countries the petty bourgeoisie, or this very extensive middle-class patchwork, is not a residual category but the majority.

Inside this group there is a split between modernist and traditionalist tendencies. Laroui also identifies two types of intellectual: eclectic and traditionalist.[7] But in Iran's case these two types need to be subdivided in other ways, for they are by no means homogeneous groups. One may be faced with a secular intellectual of left or right; an intellectual educated in Western style but keen to restore traditional values (a sort of nostalgic Muslim version of the counter-culture); someone who wants to reconcile Islam with modernity, like the enlightened Islamic tendency of Mehdi Bazargan; an Islamic ideologue eager to overthrow the established order to hasten the socio-messianic revolution (the People's Mojahedin); or a fundamentalist fanatic of Hezbollah type. It is quite clear that the categories are not sufficiently defined. There are a number of dualisms which cut across one another at different levels. There is a dualism of education between those with direct access to modern knowledge and those who are dependent on translations; there is an ideological dualism between progressives and traditionalists. The progressives may belong to either educational group (with direct or indirect knowledge of the West), just as traditionalists may be people who have received a modern training abroad, like most of the bearded 'Islamic' technocrats whose qualifications were earned in the United States.

Whatever the ideological makeup of the intellectuals, their education, their political leanings, their ambivalent relationship with Tradition, they are placed between the two structured poles of Iranian society: the *technocrats* (among whom I include all professionals and scientists) and the *ulemas*. The same dualism is reflected in the various institutions of learning. The scientific institutes train engineers, doctors, technocrats for both public and private sectors; men of letters (in the very broadest sense) supply the universities and humanities faculties, whose considerable surplus output — consisting largely of potential unemployed — finds work in the various state organizations (many intellectuals used to work in the planning ministry while others were officials of cultural organizations, for example) while continuing to exercise the vocation of intellectuals on a part-time basis.

Such is the prestige of technical skills that the most able pupils compete for places in the technical and medical schools; the less gifted find their way into the humanities faculties, emerging after several years of study to become intellectuals who double as civil servants. The number of genuinely independent intellectuals — people who are not employed by the state in any capacity — is quite small. At the other end of the spectrum are the religious institutions where mullahs are trained, which have preserved their medieval structure more or less intact. This ensures a dualism between two radically opposed academic worlds, between which there stretches a whole nuanced range of different cultural contaminations.

Because they are caught between two fires — technocrats on one side, *ulemas* on the other — intellectuals are in a very exposed position. They are also the most directly influenced by all the distortions contaminating the field of knowledge. Unknowingly Westernized in the content of their tendentiously ideological discourse, making indiscriminate use of all the half-digested ideas floating in the air, extremely militant and active, they are the most ardent promoters of every ideological deformation. They have the resentful arrogance of people being flayed alive. A large book could be written on the phenomenology of resentment as it applies to this particularly frustrated group of intellectuals. The resentment is a product of multiple frustrations: dissatisfaction with the education system and the lack of access to foreign languages, envy of those who have studied abroad or, among those who have, the memory of life in a relaxed, liberated, non-religious environment, where, for example, they could associate freely with the opposite sex. Such lingering resentments embitter their comportment, which reaches a peak of venomous aggressiveness when they are belabouring scapegoats. These take many different forms: sometimes the target is the repressive system in the service of foreign enemies; sometimes the technocrats (those native colons and lackeys of imperialism) grinding the faces of the 'wretched of the earth'; sometimes the depraved and gilded offspring of the privileged classes whose talk is spiced with incomprehensible foreign buzzwords (and who are therefore alienated from their own culture); and sometimes of course it is the pervasive and pernicious Great Satan, censorship, destroyer of all creative impulses.

There is of course an element of truth in all this, but to vent hostility on these phenomena without trying to analyse the complex reasons for them is to give superficial attention to a problem whose lower depths conceal important material. And when later, as a result of the exile and dispersal of Iranians, many of these restrictions were lifted, nothing worthy of attention was produced. The very fact that after such an abrupt and far-reaching change of system the same restrictions reappeared, but on an even more overwhelming scale, suggests mimetic comportment derived from cultural models which are deeply rooted in the collective psyche. Any comprehensive explanation must certainly take this into account.

A Double Claustrophobia

The group of mediocre intellectuals, undoubtedly the most numerous, is characterized by *cultural claustrophobia*. For despite their social demands (which are often justified) and their cultural ones (which are less so), these intellectuals are usually sterile and create nothing original. The claustrophobia stems from a double impasse. On the one hand, they feel clearly superior to the mass of the people, whose historical backwardness and obscurantism they deplore (while furtively praising its infallible authenticity); on the other hand, they have a feeling of inferiority in relation to the West whose products they admire, and are well aware that despite their deafening clamour they are themselves trailing in the wake of modernity. The advantage they have on one side is therefore cancelled out on the other. Their secret, seldom-admitted ambition is to gain the acceptance of the so-called civilized world, to haul themselves up to a level of accepted universality and thus escape the debilitating provincialism in which they are buried. Hence the permanent unease and a sort of claustrophobia on two levels; hence, too, the feeling of being misunderstood which, if one is conceited (and one often is), results in a sort of corrosive cynicism. Suspended between a culture of which they are 'in advance' and the dazzling, inaccessible bright lights of a wider outside world, they remain alienated from both. The great modern Iranian writer Sadegh Hedayat (1903-51) has an excellent image for this conflictual situation when he describes himself as a 'stick gilded at each end'. Youssef Ishaghpour tells us that gold here, like gold in dreams, should be understood as an image for excrement.[8] 'Neither from here nor from elsewhere; driven from here, not arrived there.'

Existentially, intellectuals drown in stifling claustrophobia; socially too, as I have said, they are suspended between two poles of attraction: the technocracy and the *ulemas*. Pulled apart between these two worlds, the intelligentsia has neither the precise, utilitarian skills of the technocrats nor the organic, homogeneous, scholastic learning of the clergy; nor has it succeeded in establishing an autonomous status of its own by wielding the redoubtable weapon of criticism. Thus unprotected, it is at the mercy of any ideological aggression and every error of judgement. It makes no impression on· the technocrats, who look on it with scorn as underdeveloped; the clergy too, while willing to form tactical alliances with it, withhold their full acceptance. The intelligentsia's role is thus formed in the image of the hybrid world it embodies: a medium for the transmission of two heterogeneous discourses incorporating two entirely different orders of ideas, which can, however, be brought together — as actually happened — in the aggressive ideologies of militants.

Had the intelligentsia been capable of assuming its proper critical role, it would undoubtedly have been the meeting-place of these two worlds. It would have served as a bridge between the two, articulating their dialogue while keeping intact — and this is most important — the line of fracture between their conceptual backgrounds. A reflective role of this sort, adopted deliberately and without preconceptions, would have exposed the conceptual strata underlying the different bodies of knowledge, the caesuras marking the passage from one to another, the modes of perception characteristic of each discourse. In short, the intelligentsia could have organized and managed the free space of their encounter, without subjecting one to the other, highlighting their incompatible aspects as well as their fertile cross-pollinations. But it could only assume this function by remaining aloof from parochial attitudes and squabbles. The great debate on Westernization and the relationship between modernity and Tradition in Iran during the 1960s and 1970s might have been fertile, if the protagonists had refrained from confusing the two discourses with one another, if they had not been unconsciously preparing the ground for the onslaught of a new obscurantism. But by putting the cart before the horse and effectively undermining the foundations of secularism, the Iranian intelligentsia made the cardinal error of abandoning modernity in favour of a nostalgic archaism. For after the revolution the intelligentsia was literally swept away and, having failed to weather the storm, gave up and sank into a kind of clandestinity, vegetating ineffectually on the fringes of the new system.

Intellectuals in our part of the world are more like crusaders tilting at windmills than thoughtful sages reflecting in the peace of their book-lined studies. Being an intellectual in our world means, just for a start, being opposed to the régime. This is understandable since most of the régimes in place are at least repressive and often nakedly totalitarian. But unfortunately this opposition remains coarse and visceral, unaccompanied by critical analysis, by an objective, distanced attitude or any coherent perspective. The opposition rises against the régime as an individual would rebel against his father or mother. The régime's cultural context is not taken into consideration, the basic questions are not even formulated. Why this régime rather than another? Why do the same models go on stubbornly and remorselessly recurring? How does it happen that the most laudable efforts are always doomed to failure? Where does it come from, this repeated failure, proof against all defences, infallible cause of derailment after derailment? Analysis of the socio-economic factors — almost standard practice since the instruments were provided by vulgar Marxism — is not sufficient. The overthrow of the old order by a revolution is not, alas, equivalent to setting up a more equitable order. Far from it. According to Gaston Bachelard:

> First and foremost you have to know how to formulate problems. Say what you like, problems do not formulate themselves in the world of science. This *sense of problem* is the defining mark of the scientific spirit. To a scientific mind, all knowledge is an answer to a question. If there was no question, there could be no scientific knowledge. Nothing is self-explanatory. Nothing is given. All is constructed.[9]

This sense of problem, fundamental for understanding the fate of our countries, has only rarely been deployed by our intellectuals, not through bad faith but because they were simply too blinkered to be capable of it. They lacked both the long-range perspective and the knowledge. What they said, what they thought, was always out of context: unconnected with the historical conditions of the country, the misery of a disoriented culture reduced to a self-caricature; unaware of the centuries spent on the sidelines, on holiday, during the great changes shaking the world; and without any say in the destiny of the planet which was being decided elsewhere. All these questions, if raised knowingly and addressed with intelligence, might have altered the intellectual topography of the country, changed the political perspective of debate, and raised the intellectual to his rightful, privileged rank: that of an element in the objectivized consciousness of society.

I am of course setting aside those poets, major writers and genuine researchers whose products are remarkable in many ways but remain unknown in the outside world, mainly because the language in which they are written has sadly become an isolated local tongue, without influence on the great literary creations of the planet. Translations into foreign languages are extremely rare, and when the work of poets — undoubtedly the richest creative writers of the Iranian world — is involved the problem is almost insoluble, as the language of poets is untranslatable by definition.

But even poets and great artists are not immune to the damaging presence of distortions of all sorts, and to the lack of critical sensibility characteristic of these civilizations. When they try to deal with socio-philosophical problems, for example, they launch into ideas of a mind-numbing banality or lose themselves in pointless and interminable discussions. The divorce between creative talent and critical faculty opens the fracture in the depths of our being into a yawning gulf. It has nothing to do with the artist's talent or lack of discernment but is due to something deeper: the metaphysical incompatibility between the different worlds which are present. The artist's own world has no suitable response to the endlessly jostling and changing problems posed by a modernity in perpetual mutation. However devastating his irony, however skilfully he may juggle, ridicule, dodge, quibble and equivocate, he cannot evade the gross reality of the questions arising from an altogether difficult daily experience. So he is forced to seek arguments elsewhere: in the context of the 'modern' human sciences where everything can be linked up according to a more or less rigorous system. Intuition, spontaneity, the large metaphysical answers favoured by Oriental doctrines, are no longer sufficient — at least where historical problems are concerned. For these you have to know things, you have to be up to date, have a certain perspective, a certain objective distance: you have to be informed. You have to know what you are talking about, what you are referring to, what context you are talking in; in other words you need qualifications, intellectual luggage, clear ideas, precise notions, defined postulates; firm ground, an ontological base. To be a Marxist is to be put instantly on a certain wavelength, a world organically linked to earlier philosophies. Marx is not the result of some kind of spontaneous generation but is a product of the whole ontology of the West from Aristotle onwards. Nobody is going to understand anything about the spirit of Marxism by staying up all night absorbing the Persian translation of Georges Politzer's *Principes élémentaires de philosophie*. About the best you can hope for is to become a rabid Stalinist like those formed in the Tudeh Party's underground cells during the 1940s and 1950s. It does not help to be a talented writer, a poet of genius or a blazing visionary when the problems require different intellectual tools. To analyse facts, to understand social mutations, to find one's way through the tangled world of ideas, to track down cultural references, it is necessary to be a cultivated person in the humanist sense. And this, alas, is terribly lacking among us. Our thinkers recall the Russian intellectuals of whom Berdyayev said something along these lines: 'They are either nihilists or apocalyptics. They are deficient in what comes between: the area in which cultural values are crystallized.'

The Negative Salvation of Fate
To return to the subject of the most widespread type of intellectual, we should say that a large part of the socio-political work of these intellectuals never goes beyond the local level. They seldom manage to give a cross-section of the socio-cultural splits which divide the country's sociological landscape, not to mention the psychological behaviour of its various groups, let alone their own schizophrenia. If you ask them why they were mistaken on the nature of the Iranian revolution, they will give you a thousand reasons without mentioning the essential ones: their own ignorance of the country's geopolitical situation, of the extent of fanaticism and of the cultural hand played by the clergy (who in the final analysis cared not a fig for democracy but just wanted power, pure and simple).

This incomprehension, in all its catastrophic scope, was perhaps inevitable owing to the stupid, mindlessly querulous censorship of the old régime, which predisposed people to intellectual myopia. This censorship prevented the youth from becoming aware of the stupefying mediocrity of the subversive literature circulating under the counter, whose quite unnecessary clandestine status turned it from a molehill into a mountain. Exposure of this unfounded rubbish, masquerading as revolutionary doctrine, polemical diatribes against the organs of the state, satires and messianic pamphlets, would undoubtedly have neutralized its more noxious effects and formed some kind of immunizing defence mechanism. For many intellectuals were shocked by the worrying implications of these enormities, and tried to defend the truth and bring a little order into the chaotic tumult of ideas. There were plenty of leaks and loopholes in the old régime's comprehensive surveillance system, however, so that anyone with cunning could slip his message through. The literature of the period — among the richest of modern Iran, using an elliptical and allegorical language — also lent itself to the purpose.

Besides, the Iranian intelligentsia belonged organically to the imperial system, while rejecting it emotionally. Both inhabited the same *constellation*; with the fall of the old régime the intelligentsia lost its natural adversary, its hated *alter ego*, so to speak, and its own voice was soon lost in the desert. The present régime, well out of range of its artillery, did not even take the intelligentsia seriously. The Islamic government regarded intellectuals as part of the jetsam of the old régime, or worse still as the irrecoverable debris of the depraved West.

All these errors of judgement, which whether we like it or not have become our daily portion, arise from the fact that our spirit is very old. Bachelard would say that it had reached the age of prejudice. To think is to undergo a spiritual rejuvenation, and also 'to accept a sudden mutation tending to contradict the past'.[10]

It is very hard for our intellectuals to escape from their claustrophobic cultural enclave. They have great difficulty in experiencing the catharsis of thought, in replacing their static, petrified wisdom with open, dynamic knowledge and 'at last giving reason reasons to evolve'.[11] For most of these intellectuals are doubly alienated: from the new ideas they acquire by osmosis — that is, without critical reflection — and also from the popular culture of which they retain not the essence but — let us speak plainly — the crass and unsubtle exterior. Reduced to balancing one deficiency against the other, playing an ill-defined identity off against an equally vague alienation, they are left hanging in the limbo of history, in no man's land. Their splintered thought is in the image of the culture they embody: a pseudo-culture which yells at the top of its voice but produces nothing solid, which strikes out to left and right but cannot find a spot in which to take root. There are two extreme reactions which vary with the individual's choice, one political and one existential: rage, which turns people into vengeful ideologues, or the consciousness of failure, which produces a feeling of resentment and disenchantment. At worst, this last takes on mystical overtones of sublime futility, something which has deep roots in the country's culture. Gobineau refers to this feeling with his usual perceptiveness:

After hearing it endlessly repeated that the world is worthless, even that it does not exist, that the love of wife and children is utterly false, that the sentient man should look to himself and keep to himself, placing no trust in friends who would betray him; that it is only in his own heart that he can find happiness, security, easy forgiveness for his faults, the most tender indulgence, and finally God; it would be extraordinary if most of those receiving such lessons, and seeing them universally approved, did not end by accepting as virtues the most naïve egotism and all its consequences, the most important being a complete detachment from everything going on around them in the family, in the town and in the country at large.[12]

Gobineau also thinks that the roots of the scorn these nations feel for their governments should be sought in the same area. Here he puts his finger on a sore point: should the failure of these societies be imputed solely to their governments, or should the causes also be sought among the cultural antecedents which must have shaped the recurrent structures of the collective psyche? Although the corruption and incompetence of Asiatic administrations are immense, the burdens resulting from religion, custom and morality are even more paralysing, since these are the very obstacles liable to 'halt at any moment even the legitimate actions of the authorities'.[13] Even if the leadership includes people who are both capable and well-intentioned — something which happens more often than people think — they still fail. For what 'public opinion is moved to grumble about most bitterly is any attempt at reform; it is far more irritated by these attempts than by the superannuated, rapacious and often completely senseless attitudes inherent in the old system'.[14]

Although it was made more than a century ago, this remark is not only still valid but perceptive in many ways; it exposes one of the reasons for failure. Any attempt at reform shakes up the habitual ways of doing things, disturbs the static vision of reality, demands a change of attitude and a restructuring of mentalities. It tends to elicit an atavistic resistance and a retreat towards ancient ossified models, whose pressures are borne far more cheerfully than the disorders which might result from excessively bold reforms. The reason for this is that the 'superannuated attitudes' of old systems are an integral part of the fate that weighs down on things and turns our sojourn here below into a succession of trials to be overcome. It is easier to cohabit with a familiar, domesticated despair than to entertain uncertain hopes holding out a vague promise of the moon and stars. The longer you live within your means, 'cash down' day by day, the less confidence you have in the credit of the future and the inevitable failure contained in it. Because failure, inevitable failure, is everywhere: in the inability to change the course of things, in the fact that the fate of the world is being decided elsewhere, somewhere out of reach; in these shackles hung round our necks and dragging from our ankles like heavy chains. An existential, fatal, involuntary failure justifies all frustrations, consoles the powerless, flatters personal inadequacy and causes furtive pleasure to be taken in the failure of others; so that any social or political success, even if carried with grace, even if well-merited, becomes in the final analysis a dubious achievement, something against the rules of the game.

Cioran says:

> To exempt themselves from action, oppressed peoples entrust themselves to 'fate', a negative salvation as well as a means of interpreting events: an *easy-to-use* historical philosophy, an emotionally based determinist vision, an occasional metaphysics.[15]

This negative salvation is what enables us to tolerate the cycle of failures, to resign ourselves to the inevitable, to accept an apparently meaningless existence, without lifting a finger or turning a hair. Cioran goes on:

> Whatever good will I might have mustered, would I have been able, without my country, to waste my days in so exemplary a manner? It has helped me to do so, led me on, encouraged me. To spoil one's life, one forgets all too quickly, is not so easy: it takes a tradition, long training, the labor of several generations. This labor performed, everything goes perfectly. Futility then forms part of your inheritance: it is a possession your ancestors have acquired for you by the sweat of their brow and at the cost of countless humiliations.[16] [And you get the benefit, you lucky devils. Flaunt it for all to see.]

But to be as lucid as Cioran you need to do a little more than submit to destiny: you have to be able to demonstrate that exposing its pernicious workings will free you from it, exorcise it, as it were, so that you become like the lotus in the *Bhagavad Gita* which remains unharmed and unsullied even when it is trampled in the mud.

A Hemiplegic Outlook

Oppressed peoples who consign themselves to destiny, who give up all idea of action, and who have the misfortune to live in a heterogeneous world where all the values have been displaced, eventually acquire a hemiplegic outlook. This outlook is always half paralysed: if it criticizes the other, it idealizes the self; if it attacks one thing, it sanctifies another. It cannot stay in two registers at the same time, be both questioner and provider of answers, be neither for nor against but above both, in the critical attitude inherent in all objectivity. This applies to everybody including artists and great writers.

In an open letter to Günter Grass, who had scolded him for calling

Gabriel García Márquez a courtier of Fidel Castro, Mario Vargas Llosa
says:

> I have always maintained that literary talent and intellectual brio are
> no guarantees of lucidity in political matters, and that in Latin
> America, for example, a considerable number of writers do not under-
> stand democracy, and support ideas of Marxist-Leninist persuasion to
> resolve our problems.[17]

Vargas Llosa calls this state of things *moral hemiplegia*, condemning the
injustices of military dictators and the abuses permitted by the
democracies, while shutting one's eyes to the reality of socialist régimes.
Why? Because the myth of revolution is as operational as ever and
presents itself as a panacea for all the ills of society. This illusion prevents
people from seeing the cruel realities of the Gulag, the Prague Spring, the
flight from their country of a hundred thousand Cubans, but above all it
prevents intellectuals from giving wholehearted support to the vulnerable
young democracies in their countries. Apart from this, though, the word
democracy has been prostituted by the deliberately confusing use which is
made of it. Everyone lays claim to it 'from Gaddafi to Khomeini via Kim Il
Sung and General Stroessner'.[18] If democracies could rely on the support
of their intellectuals they would be less fragile; but for fear of being
'satanized' as reactionaries, a lot of intellectuals abdicate responsibility
and play no part in attempts at democracy. Let us take the example of
Peru, whose recent democracy (established in 1980) has become a major
victim of terrorist violence: the organization spreading the terror, Shining
Path, was born not among the peasants or in the factories, but in
university circles, among teachers and students who 'never even dreamed
that their senseless justifications of violence, *"midwife of history"* and so
forth, were going to result in the bloodbath Peru is living through
today'.[19]

Vargas Llosa thinks that even the most imperfect democracies allow
intellectuals greater freedom than the least rigid socialist régimes. And
that is why, he says by way of conclusion, the sight of García Márquez
dancing attendance on the leader of a régime which has so many political
prisoners, which tolerates no criticism and drives intellectuals into exile,
is so shameful. In cases like this, the possession of a great talent is not a
mitigating circumstance but an aggravating one.

I do not understand what could have induced a writer like García Márquez to behave as he does towards the Cuban régime. His loyalty goes beyond ideological solidarity and often assumes the form of religious bigotry or adulation.[20]

Like the Peruvian writer, I too am unable to understand why some of Iran's most fashionable intellectuals, who had opposed the old régime and then ranged themselves against the new one, should have chosen to fall into the arms of another, even more intolerant guide as soon as they were out of the country. How can an intellectual worthy of the name espouse the cause of a political movement like the People's Mojahedin, a movement which functions like the maddest sort of sect, with the mystical marriage of the charismatic leader and his mistress celebrated both as a historic event and an ideological revolution? How can they swallow a therapeutic ideology which cures the mentally sick, soothes psychosomatic ills and acts, not to put too fine a point on it, like a powerful alternative to brainwashing?

That supposedly self-respecting intellectuals should swear allegiance, without plausible explanation, to a movement whose leader is regarded as the voice of the Prophet, his marriage an act of founding hierogamy, his powers (like those of medieval monarchs) thaumaturgical manifestations of charisma able to cure lepers and the possessed, all this by itself is an extremely grave pathological case. How can it be explained? To describe these intellectuals as opportunists, *arrivistes* false to the core, does not get us very far. Perhaps some are. But there are some who are really sincere, who believe in the thing with all the ardour of their ingenuous souls. That is what really hurts: how can anyone believe in such a sham? How can it be explained except in terms of the painful reality of a deep breakage which takes different forms: hemiplegic outlook, schizophrenic comportment, divorce between the mimetic archaism of fixed attitudes and the pseudo-modernity of progressive ideas. Perhaps in this (more than disconcerting) allegiance there is the cult of violence for its own sake. The bravery, the dedication, the suicidal attitude of harebrained militants, fascinate these intellectuals, who identify with them eagerly, and thus compensate for their creative castration with a transference onto extremist super-heroes whose lust for martyrdom and virile integrity become values in themselves, independent of all critical and even practical considerations. It is precisely these multiple contradictions that create the hemiplegia to which Vargas Llosa refers. Talent has nothing to do with it. It is perfectly possible to be a great writer and be cock-eyed as well.

Octavio Paz says on this subject, after pointing out that Latin America lives intellectually at *second hand*:

> After the eighteenth century we stopped dancing in time, although —
> as in the 'modernist' period — we occasionally try to copy the
> fashionable steps . . . Our inability to stay in rhythm has produced, as it
> were by accident, unique works of art: works which merit the term
> exceptional. In the domain of thought, on the other hand, and in
> politics, public morality and social affairs, our eccentricity has proved
> baleful.[21]

In the domain of thought, it is particularly important to dance in time, to be in synchronized rhythm with events, to evolve with the movements of history; otherwise an oblique displacement occurs, leading to distortions and thence to a hemiplegic outlook and a false awareness. This last reinterprets the world in terms of its own conceptual framework: it spatializes the passage of time in a finite space, where ideology hypostatizes into an *idée fixe*. Psychologically, too, the attitude of an intellectual who follows a movement religiously, or subscribes to the personality cult of some leader or other, seems to me to betray psychic immaturity: the yearning for integration of an *underdeveloped* ego which, fearing solitude and uncertainty, withdraws into the cocoon of a safe haven. Where the family is absent or inadequate this refuge might be the Clan, or failing that the Party or Sect. Once cosily installed there one can project ideas which, having no basis in fact, become masks, but masks which can be exchanged for others at any time, without tears or remorse; even with a certain careless serenity, since behind all the masks there is an anxious child afraid to leave his mother. This is also why there is so little fear of contradictions. Those who are sheltered and looked after have no need to justify themselves to anyone. Marxists on the run seek refuge in the United States or Europe and settle down happily among the massed tools of the hated capitalism; those fascinated by the sirens of Tradition pursue their studies at Berkeley or Harvard but only rarely in the theological schools of Qom or Najaf. And whatever they do, they do it innocently; they are not responsible. Responsibility is a matter for depraved adults, not for perpetual innocents playing their perpetual games in the perpetual garden of unawareness.

2
Ideologues

Having remained on the sidelines during the great historic upheavals that transformed the landscape of our planet over several centuries, the Asian and African civilizations received the resulting changes by procurement. Without access to the motive source of modernity or to its inexhaustible dialectical vitality, they were reduced to consuming its cultural by-products, including quick-frozen packages of ready-to-eat ideology. The result is that over time, ideology in all its forms has become the ultimate importable commodity, the meeting point between two worlds and the only form of thought accessible to non-Western civilizations through which they can still aspire to a historical role. But as I have said elsewhere:

As the determining structures of the ideologies are secularized, any spiritual content, once it has been poured into the mould of a closed ideological system, acquires its shape (although continuing to claim authenticity), is unconsciously Westernized and thus becomes a false awareness. This explains the extraordinary success of leftist ideologies — those most highly charged with utopianism — in the third world, bearing in mind that the innate dogmatism of ideologies adapts very well to the religious spirit of these civilizations, which can only secularize themselves through a process of ideologization; and which, because they have not lived through the scientific and technical age of the Enlightenment, because they have missed out on the adventure of history, remain resistant to the compensating antidote of a critical faculty, which in the West often counteracts dangerous excesses of dogmatization.[22]

Compared to the unhappy consciousness of the intellectual, who uses his doubt as a universal instrument for dealing with all knowledge, the ideologue has the advantage of possessing unshakeable certainties forged out of incisive *a priori* notions. Unlike the sage who is essentially placed above the material struggle and whose ultimate aim is liberation, the ideologue is concretely involved in a specific set of beliefs. He has the faith of one who believes he possesses the truth and is intolerant of anyone opposing him or disputing his monopoly of truth. At the same time, as most of our intellectuals suffer from a worrying deficiency of critical sense and tend to make sweeping judgements which completely ignore whole areas of reality, we may conclude that the dividing line between the intellectual and the ideologue is not very distinct. This is perhaps also true of Western societies, but in their case there is such a surplus of criticism in every direction that people acquire a sort of immunity to the virus of every school of thought. It is true that in Europe, too, there are loud-mouthed ideologues who quite often give vent to bizarre, deviant opinions on the burning issues of the day; but they are surrounded by quieter, more reasonable voices which usually restore the balance and prevent general contagion. It is also the case that those who aspire to leadership roles in the West are expected to cultivate their gifts, acquire knowledge, show ability and gain acceptance as responsible public figures. Among us, on the other hand, revolt — especially political revolt — is seen as a value *per se*. You can be nothing at all, and be a hero at the same time: all you have to do is enrol in the potential martyrs' club. This enables you to dispense with all effort, to do without any talent. To allow yourself to be detained by the régime for a few months is to guarantee a hero's welcome on release, followed by a dazzling social success; under these circumstances the most useless collection of ineptitudes, slung together and called a book, will sell thousands of copies. Prison becomes the essential prelude to heroic status, the golden key to social success. Of course the régime, stupid as ever, gets drawn into the game, lumbers through its own moves and cheerfully foots the bill; one would expect no less.

It could be said of our intellectuals that they are for the most part ideologues, people who are not only afflicted by all the distortions imaginable (false awareness, false assimilation, unconscious hybridization of ideas, etc) but actually want to put them into practice. For somehow the usefulness of ideas seems more pertinent than their mere theoretical formulation. Any sense of the problem in its own right, divorced from its social and political implications, seems to belong to the domain of sterile — not to say totally irrelevant — issues.

An Egocentric Consciousness
An ideologue who is excessively active by temperament can easily drift into the radicals' camp and even, under the right circumstances, become a terrorist. But not every ideologue is necessarily an out-and-out militant. He can stay out of trouble, behave in a prudent and circumspect manner, and still remain an ideologue at heart: someone who is held in the closed system of an egocentric consciousness cut off from the outside world. The ideologue flourishes best in lands where modernity is still very lame, having neither taken root nor found its way into customs and morals: in other words, in countries where the modern age arrived through procurement, and whose thinkers played no part in the festival of the great changes. That is why the ideologue dislikes the sudden mutations and metamorphoses of the age. He is anti-dialectical and anti-historical. His natural categories are the reification of outlook, the idealization of the self. When he feels threatened he sees plots everywhere, and for this reason he is also Manichaean. This characteristic is as natural to him as intellectual detachment to the sage or doctrinal tolerance to the intellectual.

The ideologue does not live in time but in space. He cannot feel comfortable until he has converted the movement of time into a frozen space where everything is in its correct place: where, say, the wicked are on the left, the good on the right, the discarded forms of the past behind, and in front a transparent future, visible right down to the immovable surveyor's stakes marking out the roads of utopia.

The ideologue believes in progress, but a predictable progress, predetermined by the decrees of a history whose innermost workings are known. A history which is so transparent that it is no longer linear, from time to time revealing 'tricks of reason', but simultaneous, happening in its length and breadth in an omniform expansion, as if all the past, present and future ages had appeared side by side on the single world stage to show themselves to him, the ideologue, the privileged spectator. Everything is familiar to him. There is *déjà vu* in his know-all fortune-teller's gaze. It gives him his tendency to identify to right and left, before and behind; the cascade of identification can link a banana with a squid, bridging time and space, across the centuries and societies. Let there just be a mention somewhere of stratified orders or groups, or a hint of social differentiation, and he sees class struggle, somewhat before the event. Let there be an allusion somewhere to some vague promise of consultation on the most anodyne matters, and he sees democracy, in embryo. Let there be an enemy to fight now, imperialism for example, and he sees how, through occult science, all its malignant mutations are precisely mapped, right from the beginning of time. For this privileged spectator is the centre of the world. With one eye he scans the distant past, with another he looks upon the future, while the third eye, like Shiva's, brings everything back to the space in the middle where all is revealed in a timeless simultaneity.

Like the mystic, the ideologue has a horror of the void. But while the mystic thirsts to annihilate himself in the universal whole, the ideologue zealously shuts himself away in sects, clans, closed and protected schools. The intellectual's sceptical split, his professional neurosis, the fragmentation of things, the disconnection of spheres, the separation of domains, the dismantling of edifices and ideas, in short the whole dissolving work of analysis, terrifies the ideologue. He is unable to remain in suspense between being and nothingness, myth and rationality; he cannot enter the spaces between without being seized with vertigo. Ambiguous situations, ambivalent positions, the solitude of individuality reduced to its own resources, traumatize him beyond measure. He must have at all costs a protective cocoon to shelter him from the demons of solitude. He also needs to be surrounded by a defensive array of familiar ideas. If not religion, then secular dogmas; if not God, then History; if not the Prophet, then the profane Saviours whose clacking wooden tongues hammer our eardrums all day long, whose dreary monochrome messages are parroted, amplified, pounded into people's heads every day by the rubber truncheons of the media. Because all he really needs are a few very simple ideas, simple but as solid as the rocks looming over a mountain landscape.

The ideologue cannot walk the razor's edge like a tightrope performer. He cannot be present simultaneously in two or more registers. The arts of nuance, subtle distinction and dialectic are repellent to him. What he really likes are clear and well-defined situations: either this, or that. Hence his reductive vision; hence too the dazzling success of a certain sort of vulgar Marxism whose apparent historical coherence binds instantly to his temperament. Class struggle! What an unhoped-for piece of luck, to be able to explain everything on the basis of this fundamental and omnipresent motor which deciphers unresolved enigmas, exposes power relations, denounces the misery of the farmers and the disdainful arrogance of the landlords, reveals the abject treachery of ministers in the pay of the universal conspiracy. Historical determinism! What a windfall to know that all is written in the movement of history, where everything is interconnected by an implacable logic, where nothing is left to chance, where once the process has started everything else follows in an irreversible progression. And how consoling it is to know that one is on the same side as the damned, the ignored, the ragged and down-at-heel; shoulder to shoulder with all the exploited victims of a bourgeoisie owned body and soul by the omnipotent cartels that control the world.

The Deification of the Means
The ideologue does not feel at ease within the frontiers of reason, and is discontented with man's incapacity to transcend phenomena. He needs primary causes, noumena, substantial realities from which to unravel the world as one unwinds a ball of yarn. Anything which justifies the deification of the means is good: People, Race, Revolution, History, Communism. Anything can acquire the dignity of a mythological truth and become a pseudo-divinity. Hence his tendency to mythologize secular ideas and hypostatize a fragment of being to turn it into a sub-totality. It is precisely this tendency that distinguishes the ideologue from the intellectual and the mystic.

The mystic — at least in his traditional form — lives in the visionary world of myths and images, which are perfectly integrated into the spiritual *meta-reality* which constitutes as it were the mental space of the so-called traditional civilizations. In effect, the splits between Psyche and Intellect, Myth and Rationality, which were products of modernity and secularization, have not yet occurred there. The co-presence of these two orders of reality is safeguarded in the mystery of Being. In the vision of a pre-Galilean mystical man, myth is just as reasonable as reason is mythical. This identification is proclaimed by Indian thought when it turns the cosmic intelligence into the First Evolution, and Islamic thought when it identifies the Angel of Revelation with the active Intelligence wielded by philosophers. The space in which these spiritual Figures appear is the active Imagination in which reason assumes a mythical form while myth becomes rational. The imagination is the place where the two orders are reconciled in the form of symbols and where the soul meets its self, its celestial counterpart.

But modernity blew all the security locks safeguarding the treasures of the soul. By despiritualizing heaven, that is by depopulating it, and by the same token repopulating an unconscious saturated with rejected material, modernity gave the *coup de grâce* to the co-presence of myth and reason. This final, doubtless inevitable separation had both fruitful and disastrous consequences. While it prepared the way for the emergence of the natural sciences, it also disturbed the psychic balance of man and made him a neurotic being. Later, in the modern age, the co-presence of the two orders of reality (myth and reason) was to be counterbalanced by the dialectic of their opposition. But as Adorno and Horkheimer tell us in their remarkable study on the dialectics of the Enlightenment, this opposition is a two-edged weapon. Myth is already reason, but reason can turn back into mythology. In other words, in a world emptied of symbolic images and deprived of dialectic, there is a natural tendency to turn reason back into myth. And it is this near-natural perversion that nourishes the ideologue's Manichaean behaviour. For he is a seeker after totality in a world reduced to the paltry dimensions of a raucous squabble around the parish pump.

To elucidate the history of this perversion, Adorno and Horkheimer relate the myth of the crafty Ulysses, who evades the occult forces of animism and the mythical powers, and escapes sacrifice by submitting to it in appearance only. This outwitting of the forces of nature may also lie at the very root of the enlightened reason of the *Aufklärung*. Ulysses asserts his ego and gets the better of nature, but nature avenges itself by turning his reason back into myth, by making his instrumentalized reason, stripped of its content, an implement in the service of the most unbridled instincts. 'The curse of irresistible progress and irresistible repression', these authors conclude.[23] So what is the way out of this blind alley of tragic dialectic? To remain balanced on the razor's edge with the aid of criticism, while avoiding the trap of any and all ideological identity. Adorno describes dialectic as 'the consistent sense of non-identity';[24] in my opinion, this could serve as the definition of the true intellectual. For unlike the mystic sage who refers to the original co-presence of myth and reason lying behind all oppositions, and the ideologue who re-mythologizes the bastard permutations of reason, the intellectual remains heroically wedded to the open sore of non-identity, refusing integration into some so-called order or submission to any collective entity, Hegelian totality or classless society, and thus defending the irreducible, unique singularity of the individual.

A Double Reduction

Between the transcendent path of the mystic sage, passing above the material struggle, and the heroic road chosen by the critical intellectual, the ideologue can only choose a hybrid solution: one which involves re-mythologizing a coarsened, blunted reason. This is why most thinkers from our part of the world are neither sages nor intellectuals, but ideologues. The ideologue has no real knowledge, just sub-knowledge. His snippets of information cobbled hastily together, his narrow views drawn with large, heavy strokes, are designed to be put into action: to inflame minds, change the face of the world, spread emotional contagion. His discourse, a well-chewed cud of regurgitated twaddle, simplified in the extreme, propagated independently of any context like an ideology diffused through the atmosphere, may be absorbed by radicals of all persuasions. In Iran, for example, everyone found something in it; even the imperial régime, wishing to elaborate the dialectic of King and People, resorted to it by calling on the services of a lot of old unfrocked Marxists.

The ready-made categories diffused in this way had a pervasive effect on people's minds, leaving prototypes in our perceptual apparatus which virtually became the new 'givens' of our understanding. All philosophical, political and social discourse could take shape only within these categories, stripped down to their colourless operational value. During the 1970s, when the discourse centring on questions of identity — return to Islam, religious identity and so on — was being grafted onto the existing ideological field, what we were seeing was the coalescence of two discourses, a marriage of opposites made necessary by the need to satisfy socio-political demands at the same time as establishing a so-called cultural identity, giving rise to the most perverse combinations.

That is how the ideologues came to formulate ready-made ideas to solve all the country's socio-cultural dilemmas. At the same time a new race of aggressive mutants made its appearance. The ideologues had several traits in common: the trivial flatness of their chopped-up knowledge, the raw emotiveness of their resentment and especially the simplistic nature of their representations of the world. Ideas were subjected to a *double reduction*: progressive categories were reduced to their operational level and traditional categories to their emotive level. The marriage between the emotiveness of the ideas and their operational cost, effected in the absence of any appropriate metaphysical restraints, enabled the concepts to spread at lightning speed.

As for the Marxist-Leninist ideologues, the most typical of the new mutant species — whose worthiest offspring are the People's Mojahedin —, they amalgamated and put into practice the ideas of the two most influential groups: Marxists and clergy. Marx was married to the Prophet, and world revolution was made a prelude to the eschatological appearance of the expected Imam (who was ardently awaiting the downfall of the régime of the arrogant). There was no longer any need to look for the Archangel Gabriel in the mythical field of the imagination, or in the prophetic dreams of sages, or in the glowing visions of prophets, because there he was, flesh and blood, face forested with beard, armed to the teeth, struggling at our side to liberate all the deprived of the world.

3
Technocrats

In general terms, technocrats are the managers of the technical, political, economic and scientific spheres of a modern society. They are powerful because they programme production and the ways in which it is used. They also take on the depersonalized, neutral quality of the world for whose efficiency they are responsible. They symbolize pure function stripped of all personal connotations. And like the technical and bureaucratic rationality whose order they represent, they are indifferent to the ethical purposes of what is produced. It matters little to them whether the factory they supervise is making guns for arms dealers, precision instruments for research laboratories or baby food. The technocrat thus represents captive reason in the service of production, an instrumentalized reason in which concepts emptied of their content have become simple formal envelopes.[25] This is also the reason for the technocrat's professional indifference to the ideological aims of the state or of the organization of which he is a component. This is not to suggest that he is depoliticized in any way, just that the specificity of his function absolves him of the need to adopt an ideological position. He can be used just as effectively by one political system as by another. For structurally he need only be efficient, useful and productive, nothing else. His emotional condition, the psycho-cultural and political dimensions of his personality, hardly come into it.

The technocrat tends to stay in touch with the current ideology or ideologies: without being opportunistic, he nevertheless picks up the atmosphere by osmosis. For example, the secret police of the Iranian old régime, the Savak, easily became the new régime's Savama; apart from the dismantling of a few ultra-sensitive departments, most Savak officials managed without too much difficulty to move their rifles to the other shoulder, as it were. Much the same happened in the National Iranian Oil Company (NIOC) where, apart from one or two spectacular sackings on the highest level,˙the team of technocrats running the enterprise remained almost intact. This does not mean, however, that technocrats have no personal political preferences, or that their ideological convictions cannot change from one régime to another. For example, although the technocrats of the old régime exercised the same functions as those of today (who have voluntarily joined the Islamic Republic), they had different attitudes to culture, history and the West. They were pro-Western, and nostalgic about the country's classical and pre-Islamic culture, while the new lot shows a marked interest in religious culture and is sternly anti-Western — at least in appearance.

Apart from this, the function of technocrat shows flagrant disjunctions from other spheres, especially the governmental and cultural ones (Daniel Bell[26]), even in modern societies. For these different spheres have different rhythms of change, and the hidden, sometimes gross discordances between them are responsible for the various contradictions of society. The more the function is stripped of its emotional, cultural, juridical content, the closer it is to the abstract domains of mathematics and technology, the more neutral it becomes in terms of goals, and therefore the more easily exploited by ideologies of every kind. The technocrat is in natural contradiction with the jurist, whose abiding interest is in freedom and equality, and is also opposed to the intellectual, whose job is precisely to expose the ravages caused by the technocrat's work: the alienation and depersonalization resulting from the pitiless levelling effect of the forces of production.

These tensions cause discomfort even in the countries where capitalism first appeared and developed; transported to different cultural areas, they cause earthquakes, upsets and even violent conflicts. For here the three spheres are neither well defined nor well articulated, and they do not have autonomous status or benefit, as they do in the West, from a sort of balance of forces. Here the cultural sphere has such a globalizing presence that it eclipses the other two, greatly hampering their operation in the process. In Islamic countries where religion has metastases everywhere, and where everything contrary to its spirit is officially forbidden (or nipped in the bud by self-censorship), the cultural sphere ends by paralysing everything. Here, religion seeks to Islamize the economy in the same way as it manages the social and juridical field in obedience to God's law. In a way the work of modernity in these countries, from the very beginning, has been the gradual establishment of the techno-economic and juridical spheres despite the tentacular omnipresence of the religious culture.

These days, even the countries which are most resistant to innovations cannot do without some of the rudiments of industrialization, at least in the military domain. There are thus technocrats everywhere, people who in the context of the technical and utilitarian functions they carry out are a lot more efficient, and even a lot more scrupulous, than intellectuals. For although the technocrat's function is limited, as we were saying earlier, to the deployment of an instrumentalized reason, the intellectual is not really up to the performance of his task: that of criticism.

An Ambivalent Position on Cultural Issues
The technocrat is ambivalent about culture; he is attracted and repelled by it at the same time. His scientific and technical training has the particular characteristic, especially in countries like ours where such training flies in the face of all tradition, that he can reject culture with contempt, or just as easily fall into an attitude of naïve admiration, even an unconditional adulation of the most ridiculous aspects of the so-called culture, now reduced to a sort of picturesque, folklore level. Are not some technocrats seen to admire and heap praise on all traditional phenomena, even the most obviously harmful ones? Do they not tirelessly seek the mirages of the past, intoxicated with the mystique of the desert; do not their frequent pilgrimages take them to one mosque to pray, another to prostrate themselves; to an indiscriminate acceptance of the folklore Camelot, smoking the nargileh, taking opium, reciting verses, rejoicing in the vertiginous prowess of every kind of mystifier?

For the technocrat, like his colleagues the intellectual and the ideologue, is not a coherent being but is made up of splintered fragments of desire, scattered packages of awareness, crumbs of contradictory wishes pulling this way and that, right and left, each in its own direction. Like the intellectual, the technocrat is deficient in critical spirit; but as he is a professional, involved for good or ill in the management of some enterprise or in the arcana of bureaucratic activity, he has some sense of reality and quite often knows what he is talking about. Here too, however, preconceived ideas of a certain model of development can put him grossly out of phase with the real capacity of the country in which he lives.

The technocrat, after all, like the intellectual and the cleric, is a victim of patching and grafting. He seeks to graft models of development or productivity on to his local environment which unfortunately 'take' only with the greatest difficulty. His love of figures, statistics and quantitative criteria, his concrete achievements, make him a being apart: real and unreal at the same time. Real, because there are many technical accomplishments to his credit; unreal, because one still has the impression that all these works, erected at great speed as if with a wave of the magic wand, are somehow not at the centre of things despite their imposing appearance; that they are illusory, unconnected with the personality of the country, and have no effect on the basic constitution of things. Somehow the country, both touched and spared by the vulgar opulence of all this papier-mâché scenery, sets its face ironically against change, remains resistant to the new panorama, accepts no part of it. As if, however far you went, whatever you did, however many innovations you introduced, you always ended up at the starting point: at a place which is not anywhere. This inertia is not a question of customs or culture, it is *metaphysical*, in all the immaterial opacity of unchangeability, part of the very substance of a supra-real world in relation to which all realities and events, if they exist at all, are only simulacra of reality and imitations of events.

The technocrat, as one of the mainstays of production, embodies the process which should get inertia moving, fertilize the mind and launch change. Hence the idea of development which is the technocrat's most natural function. He should be able to disinter whole slabs of unknown reality, uncover entire zones of being, generate whole areas of new contradictions. Development is to the technocrat as writing is to the intellectual. Without development, which implies productivity and linear functioning, the technocrat has no reason to exist. He can only act in a world in which things are moving and in which industry and production are matters of daily importance. And since all the societies on the planet evolve in one direction or another, he knows that his services are indispensable. The technocrat may be a believer or an atheist, espouse this or that ideology, but — whatever he says or does — his actions affect traditional culture, if only because of the foreign nature of his function. For he is 'Westernized' to the marrow, however vehemently he may assert the contrary. His knowledge is all more or less modern and, like it or not, he is one of modernity's mainstays. Whence his ambivalence towards the 'indigenous' intellectual, especially when the latter is a pure product of the soil: his attitude is tolerant, curious in a superficial way, but only rarely is he genuinely interested. Except when he falls under the spell of Tradition, changes sides completely and becomes a man possessed, disconnected from reality, driven by sublime nostalgia and regressing endlessly to the dawn of one new start after another. In the magical circles we live in, nobody is safe from accidents of this sort.

The Hopelessness of Nostalgia

Although steeped in his function, the technocrat keeps the culture of his country at a distance. His idea of culture is abstract, lordly, substantial, without any apparent link with the misery of the people who embody it. He is scornful of the country's present culture but greatly values the treasures inherited from the past, the great creations of earlier times in poetry, painting and *belles-lettres*. The present culture, which he sees as a decadent mass of trumpery, he regards with disdain: so he is proud of the great creations of the past while ceaselessly lamenting the present. He knows that behind it there are several centuries of slow disintegration, of silence, of political disenchantment; that since the arrival of modernity his patrimony has remained outside history; that at this very moment reserves drained to the lees are being further exhausted, and that the springs which once replenished them dried up long ago; and he knows how utterly crucial it is to root out the obscurantism which gnaws like gangrene through a world reduced to a shadow of itself, discouraging all real change and inhibiting all new awareness.

The more nationalistic individuals hopefully fix on a salutary *Iranism* as a viable alternative to the backwardness of Islam (that religion of primitive Bedouins from Arabia, quite incapable of restoring an old civilization to the privileged status it always enjoyed in history). These are the nostalgics. Their dreams are focused on the great empires of Persia before the Arab invasion, an event which for them marks the fatal commencement of all misfortunes. Although the more cynical sort of technocrat disdains the anachronistic aspects of society and looks upon them with sovereign contempt, the nostalgics are always sighing over the ruins of the great empires of olden times. This mooning over the distant past, this fetishization of a culture of which people are extremely proud (without having the faintest idea of how to link it with the present state of things), is not, incidentally, exclusive to this class, but a common Iranian characteristic.

Gobineau noted it, for example, more than a hundred years ago:

The Persians . . . are a very old nation, perhaps, as they themselves claim, the oldest in the world to have had regular government and to have occupied the territory in the manner of a great people. This truth is present in the minds of all members of the Iranian family. It is not just remembered and expressed by the literate classes; people of the lowest sort are full of it, eagerly refer to it and bring it into their ordinary conversation. This is the basis of the firm conviction of superiority which is one of the ideas they have in common, and an important segment of their moral heritage. I have often been complimented with the remark that the French (so far as it is possible to know) were the most notable ancient monarchy of Europe, and thus resembled the Persians. In the minds of my interlocutors, it contained a courtesy to me and a reminder of their own great glory; for in ranking my people above the other Europeans, they gave me clearly to understand how much greater was the distance between my people and themselves.[27]

There is little exaggeration here. The Persian has a very flattering idea of himself. While Indians speak tenderly of their homeland as Mother India and the Japanese with pride of their Land of the Kamis, the Persian believes himself the legitimate heir of Cyrus and Darius, and thus superior to all his neighbours. His cult of the Great Sovereigns and the Glorious Dynasties, his hyperbolic self-image as part of a Great People planted there since the beginning of time, bear witness to his historical arrogance. None of this prevents him on other occasions from being masochistic and attributing to himself all the defects under the sun, which may, he believes, represent the other side of the coin. But the fact of his uninterrupted presence and identity across a wide geographical space for more than three thousand years gives him a sense of grandeur and continuity. In the course of founding empires, being crushed under their collapsing weight, surging back out of the rubble and metamorphosing into other forms, the Persian created a world extending well beyond the present frontiers of Iran: the signs are present all over central Asia, Afghanistan and the Indian subcontinent. But if he sees everywhere the vestiges of his past, his rebirth is nowhere to be found. For a hundred years now, he has known that he has no great destiny. So he lives in a cocoon of nostalgia. In a way he resembles a Spaniard or a Russian.

> It is almost impossible to talk to a Spaniard about anything but his country, a closed universe that is the subject of his lyricism and his reflections, an absolute province, outside the world. Alternately exalted and downcast, he turns his morose and dazzled eyes upon Spain; being drawn and quartered is his form of rigor. If he allows himself a future, he does not really belong in it. His discovery: the somber illusion, the pride of despair; his genius: the genius of regret.[28]

Like the Spaniard, the Persian suffers from 'the genius of regret' and nostalgic despair, but in the manner of fatalistic peoples he is resigned to his destiny, convinced from the very beginning of the uselessness of action, of the endless cycle of recurrent failure. A creature of the periphery, he arrives too late at the banquet of history even when he makes a spectacular entrance; he cripples himself in an apocalyptic frenzy which corresponds to the disproportionate scale of his dreams. Scion of an imperial people which once drank life to the dregs, the Persian still has a hangover. Almost wholly devoid of the means to put his megalomaniac plans into effect, he is out of touch with himself. Self-critical, but indulgent towards his own faults, he accuses and forgives himself in the same breath; he wants everyone to be as he is himself, incapable of living up to his own aspirations. He is scornful of his conquerors but does everything possible to equal them. Although he disdains the Arab, he devotes all his genius to enriching Arab thought and Arab culture. What is more, he sets an example by putting into effect his own inverted nationalism in the name of the despised conqueror's religion.

Deep down, he is interested in nothing but his country, its history, its poets. How well he actually knows them is of little importance: the very fact of their existence is sufficient reason for his admiration. Chauvinistic to the point of neurosis, he admires the Imam only because he was the son-in-law of Persia,[29] Plato because he was the disciple of Zoroaster, the Prophet because he was initiated by Salman the Persian, and Christ — in the case of certain modern nationalists — because he was another incarnation of Mithra. Inclined to egocentrism, he reverts habitually to essential questions. The same dreams haunt him, the same solutions spring to his mind, but this megalomania is accompanied by a profound cynicism. He is a man possessed, but one who is often lucid. Suspended between tragedy and farce, he switches cheerfully from one to the other, from laughter to tears. Projecting his faults onto his leaders, he hates them because they resemble him too closely. Trapped between resignation and rage, he passes directly from the most benighted apathy to all-consuming apotheosis. The transitional space, where balance is possible, does not suit him except when he is exercising the arts of opportunism. For he excels in surviving distress. He acts only in sudden jerks, violent heaves, increasingly desperate leaps; with the regrettable consequence of inevitable accidents of growth and bitter regret for lost opportunities.

To return to the subject of technocrats, it should be noted that, in the Iranian case, this class of initiates to the technological disciplines of the modern age has remained on the fringes of the intelligentsia proper. Under the old régime it adopted a withdrawn attitude: it was in the country but outside it, it performed its tasks while remaining detached. It thought in its own way, but always acted outside the main currents of thought. It took little interest in 'local products' which it regarded as the clinker or waste of an underdeveloped culture. It is true that when the revolution came this class eventually took sides against the régime it embodied, but it did so through a mimetic process. While wishing for political liberation, it did not really think it possible. While working for the downfall of the régime, it did not really want it in its heart of hearts. A corner of destiny bore down on this class and forced it to acknowledge the painful irony that nothing good can be achieved, that everything went bad long ago and there is not the slightest hope of changing the natural course of things; that there is an unbridgeable gulf between the conditions prevailing in the country and any modern way of improving them. Unable to adjust its lucidity to the refractory conditions in the country, too intelligent to act in a primary fashion, and above all too withdrawn to perceive that by turning its back it was effectively undermining the basis of its own existence, it could only — fatally — abdicate responsibility.

Not only did the technocrats remain on the fringes of society and abstain from active participation in the country's intellectual life, but they were not even able to defend their personal views (although these were valid and in touch with modernist currents). Their abdication from the domain — a large one representing a wide spectrum of interests — in which they were sure to get a respectful hearing, left the centre of the stage open to invasion by ignorant petty intellectuals: people able to pronounce on all subjects with the shameless assurance of those who know very little but are not aware of the fact.

4
Strategists of God

The course of the Iranian revolution, an event which so far has proven unique in the third world, has raised with exceptional urgency a question which, in the late twentieth century, seems entirely new: the political resurgence of a caste of Priests hitherto thought to have been neutralized or at least tamed by the planetary triumph of secularism. As the seizure of power by the clergy has now been shown to be possible, what would happen if, for example, the brahmans of India set out to do the same thing, or if the Catholic Church decided to revive the Inquisition, or if the sacred in some shamanistic form returned everywhere to daily life, not as a spiritual phenomenon but as an organized body determined to oversee every area of activity? I believe that the Iranian case deserves particular attention because, whatever the initial form taken by the political intrusion of the sacred into the material world, it must inevitably develop along the same lines as in Iran.

The *ulemas* have always had enormous influence in Iran. Some respected historians believe that this state of things has historical antecedents: that the *ulemas* are in some sense the Shiite Islamic version of the priestly caste (the *Mobadan*) which existed under the Sassanids in pre-Islamic Iran. Although continuity between the two phenomena has not been demonstrated, I believe nevertheless that the Iranian clergy, unlike the *ulemas* in Sunni Islam, closely resembles a sort of caste with its own established institutions, with widespread metastases and a communications network. Not only has the clergy kept intact its visceral links with the people; its hold over the masses — especially the illiterate masses who make up the bulk of the population — is proverbial. The failure to recognize the vast scale of this latent fanaticism or to predict its exploitation by the mullahs is largely responsible for the delusions harboured by most Iranians, especially the intellectuals, on the nature of this revolution.

The mullahs, as they are familiarly called (not without a touch of irony), have a direct influence on the crowds. They are masters of psychological control, men sensitive to the whole palette of emotions and the spectrum of sentiment from banal anecdote to the storms of pathos and tragedy. They can make a mob laugh, move it to tears, excite it, mobilize it, use evocative sorcery to plug it into the mythical strata of its collective unconscious, and thus lead it into perilous and improbable adventures. The source of this power is the fact that the clergy remains on the same wavelength as the people. Culturally, both are *pre-modern*. Their models of reference, their memory, move in the same orbit; clergy and people both evolve in the same constellation. They understand each other because they live in the same epoch; they are mental contemporaries.

The mullah is the verbal expression of the people, the externalization of its internal world. What one thinks, the other says; what one wants, the other puts into effect. This long-established symbiosis, based on collusion, does have historical antecedents. For centuries the mullahs were the exclusive holders of knowledge, both in the traditional schools (*maktab khaneh*) and on the more sophisticated and learned level of the higher schools of theology (*madrasseh*) in the urban centres. Thus for many centuries they were the country's main intelligentsia, until the late nineteenth century when, under the increasing influence of the West, secular thinkers inspired by the Enlightenment began timidly to make their appearance. At first these were designated *monawar ol-fekr* (enlightened thinker) and later came to be called *rowshanfekr* (the Persian equivalent of an enlightened thinker); this term became more or less a synonym for intellectual.

A World in which Nothing Moves

These days modernity is a patent and inescapable reality. It changes things, turns them upside down, disturbs everything; but it also arouses atavistic resistances, and sometimes has the paradoxical effect of strengthening the role of those it should be sweeping aside. In the face of these destabilizing intrusions, the mullahs offer the refuge — and what a reassuring one it is! — of a Tradition where nothing moves, where everything stays bolted to its patch of ground, where all situations are culturally predictable and therefore controllable. For the contribution of religion lies not only in the dogmatic certitudes which help counteract the disturbing effects of novelty, but even more in the way it makes situations predictable, along familiar lines marked out since the beginning of time. Nothing is left to chance, nothing is left to the caprice of the moment or inflected by a passing change of mood; everything is catalogued in advance, listed in the archives from time immemorial. Religion and its illustrious representatives reassure because they always know the answer, because they push back the unknown, relegate chance to the zone of the useless, clear it away from the shining path of deliverance.

In a world where questions are disturbing and upsetting, ready-made answers are a real blessing. There are no problems whose solutions are unknown to the mullahs, no treasures to which they do not hold the key. For they represent the canons of Wisdom, of the knowledge transmitted by the Tradition (*naqli*) and the Sciences of the Intellect (*'aqli*) derived from Revelation. Basically all science, whatever its origins, is legitimate only if it is rooted in the revelations crystallized in the Book (Quran). Hence the supreme importance of the Book, of the Prophet who received and transmitted it and of those who, in the absence of the Prophet, are its Guarantors (Imams) in the context of Shiism. And who but the mullahs has access to these sources? This hierarchy of knowledge, packaged and bundled with such practised skill, contains everything capable of being known or revealed; only those destined to do so, using the appropriate methods, can gain access to what remains hidden, and therefore esoteric, behind appearances. This world, broken down into 'packages of knowledge', has a terminology of its own which is far more rigorous than the stammerings of intellectuals as they strive in vain to locate and specify their thought processes. It has its own watertight conceptual apparatus, its own well-defined categories. It is an extremely well-ordered world which has the great advantage of being superbly static, immobile as the pyramids.

A world, in fact, which is sheltered from metaphysical insecurities. All the problems were solved centuries ago. We know how God revealed His Theophanies, unfolded His Methods, deployed His Names, manifested His Attributes. We know where mankind comes from, and the nature of the sacrosanct Alliance which binds man to his all-powerful Master. We know too why man went astray, and especially we know how to prepare him for death, set him straight in the saddle for the last journey. We even tell him what to say in Arabic to the two Angels of Death when he meets them. All this knowledge has been studied and gone over with minute and endless patience. Meticulous exegeses have exposed the workings of its deepest and most obscure details; poets have sown its seeds in the four corners of the globe. And everyone has drawn from it, each according to his capacities, each according to his allotted share. Nobody is excluded, least of all the faithful. Thus this age-old body of wisdom never innovates, never leaves the beaten path but accumulates on the spot, piles up in an infinity of layers to the point of total sclerosis. In this state of pure, almost mineral inertia it has no equal in thought other than eternity. It contains no surprises, no thunderbolt *eurekas*, nothing which has not been heard and said already, a world of *déjà vu* which initiates find wherever they look. Hence the commentaries on commentaries on commentaries . . .

For it must be understood that what remains hidden is not the unknown, but the known. The unknown is a concept valid only to those who do not know that everything is inexorably known, provided you know how to approach things and whom to ask: the guardians who jealously protect the secrets of knowledge, the exclusive holders of the sacred answers. The mullah has all the answers; this makes him superior to those around him. He is learned in the innate science deriving directly from the sources of revelation. The mullah has direct access to the science of the last prophet, who was the last link in an unbroken chain of revelations stretching back to Adam, the prototype of humanity. He is thus the Repository of a religion superior to all others, Judaism and Christianity included. A well-known *hadith* puts it concisely: 'The *ulemas* are the heirs of the prophets.' This reassuring belief gives the Muslim the full measure of his own metaphysical superiority.

In this static world people know exactly what they are talking about, what they are referring to, where they are in relation to the frame of reference. This generally pre-Galilean world contains everything to do with man from his pre-natal state to the resurrection. It has its own cosmology and its own co-ordinates, and remains unaffected by the three great shocks — cosmological, biological and psychological — which, in Freud's words, have forged the consciousness of modern man. Somehow these great upheavals of the modern age have not displaced man in the cosmos, have not evicted him from his original dwelling, have not dismantled his prophetic genealogy, have not exposed the troubled waters of the irrational or the weak links in reason; have not, in short, even touched the magnificent mental isolation of these happy beings.

The mullahs live — or at least used to before the revolution— in a protected enclosure which, like a waking dream, floats above the dangers and devastation of the world stage, suspended above the slippery slopes of reality. Its spirit is well illustrated by an amusing and bizarre — but true — anecdote. When the American Apollo mission landed on the moon and mankind set foot there for the first time, the zealous students of a school of theology in Iran hurried with the news to their master, a very venerable ayatollah. To their surprise the old man looked extremely displeased and growled, 'So you believe all the rubbish peddled by the Western press?' The students assured him that this news was true, and swore by all the Imams that they had with their own eyes seen the images on television. The master became more stubborn than ever. 'This thing has no intelligible cause,' he concluded. 'And why not? Because the terrestrial sphere cannot be penetrated.' The pupils were so flabbergasted that one of them ventured to ask whether 'the miraculous powers of the mystics who crossed the stormy oceans on foot' had an intelligible cause. 'Yes!' the master replied simply.

While hardly giving a fair impression of all the ulemas (some of whom are very well informed), this story does explain a number of things, starting with the semantic import of the term 'intelligible cause' (dalil-e 'aqli) which has different connotations in different cultural contexts. The cause or reason at issue — in this context the two categories are confounded — is one still impregnated with the aura of the earliest cosmogonies. It is a reason which depends not on man but on divine authority. Its originating power is so great that it transcends the illusion of our perception — our having seen images on television. The world is not as we believe we see it, but as it appears in the light of the divine Intellect.

The mullahs see everything in this light: that is why, when moving between their mental universe and everyday reality, one is constantly falling over abrupt disjunctions. It would all be quite harmless, even picturesque, if they had remained separate from the régime. But when they arrived flat-footed in the arena of action, what had once been an idyllic, charming quality was sadly revealed as an embarrassing defect. Their mimetic intelligence trained in the ruses of survival, adapted to the maintenance of inertia rather than to innovation, was put severely to the test. In order to survive they were now obliged to innovate, to go against the spirit of their caste, to act against their own nature. Trapped in a course of events they failed to foresee, dragged against their better judgement into an unpredictable adventure, they present the acrobatic spectacle of men forced to perform two contradictory roles at once: pyromaniacs and firemen, extinguishing the flames spread by their own crashing entrance on to the political stage.

Of course not all mullahs have enjoyed the same educational benefits. Like other such groups they include genuine sages, men who are less learned, and ignoramuses. This last group, which unfortunately is the largest, has a thoroughly baleful influence on the masses. Most of the people are not provided with modern education, especially in the rural areas, and get a large part of their knowledge orally from village mullahs. Their days fall into the rhythm of prayer, they piously imitate the gestures of holy Imams, cling to illusions of the Beyond and live in trembling terror of hell. The more afraid they are of being in a state of sin, the easier they are to influence and manipulate. This situation is now undergoing a profound change.

The reason why the mullahs were always able to mobilize the masses is that, apart from their adherence to the same cultural constellation, they were on the same side of the barricades facing a régime (the modern state and its lay institutions) which seemed equally hostile to both. By showing themselves to be defenders of the faith, the mullahs were able to support the people against excesses by the secular régime, especially as the over-hasty reforms of the modern state tended to cut people off from the religion which gave them cultural security. But when the mullahs found themselves on the other side of the barricades, everything changed. In taking over the institutions of the modern state, they were forced to submit to its implacable logic, bow to its imperious demands, embrace the alienation which goes with all power. The scapegoat on which all opposition had been focused for so long had abruptly disappeared: the wicked were no longer right there, behind desks and counters, in the police stations and standing guard outside palaces and ministries, but somewhere undefined, hidden in a semi-mythical elsewhere, in the form of Satans great and small, hatching God knows what threatening plots. The oppressed, who had once shown themselves such wholehearted defenders of the people's religious rights, now became oppressors of a most frightening kind, promising nothing but ruin, martyrdom and desolation. Even the holy Imams were involved, for they were no longer cherished mysterious dream-figures but militants who sometimes became vulgarly visible. They could even be seen, angels of death wrapped in white veils, walking the battlefields in the evening to console the parched dying.

The First Waves of Modernity

Mullahs in the popular imagination have a reputation for indifferent quality. There is a rich variety of pejorative expressions cataloguing their vices and defects, vilifying, mocking and insulting them. It is significant that the new Persian literature of the early twentieth century started with satirical treatment of these negative qualities. Every profession becomes a shopkeeping exercise in the long run, and mullahs have acquired by professional deformation characteristics which are semi-innate: the certainty that they alone possess the truth, the arrogance resulting from this same imagined sufficiency and an immovable obstinacy which verges on the indecent. There are of course many exceptions. I have had the opportunity to meet exceptional men of very great spiritual quality. I learned a great deal from some of them and was often surprised by their openness and tolerance on many matters. But even in these cases I could not help noticing a certain rigidity. Underlying their honest, open attitude there was a rejection of the other, as if their faith required them to remain intolerant, to oppose any thought which might disturb their internal security. Added to these traits was an excessive caution and a patent lack of trust in their neighbours. Dissimulation (*taqqiya*), a habit inherited from their remote predecessors, has become their second nature. Their openness has its limits and their sincerity, even when they are being overwhelmingly familiar, never comes from the depths of their being. Somewhere inside themselves, behind the veneer of seductive forms, they remain inaccessible to all attempts at contact.

When the first waves of modernity rolled over the country at the beginning of the century during the Constitutional movement, their discourse became more radical because, for the first time, they found themselves at grips with threatening ideas which had no clear representation in their minds. Accustomed to survival in all circumstances, to keep afloat at all costs in times of adversity, they took advantage of their prestige to adapt to the new situation by trying to range themselves alongside those demanding change (there were some notable exceptions, to whom we will return later). But they did not just have to face the challenge of modernity; it was preceded by another, more traditional challenge, one with a very long past in the country's history. Theologians had always had to cope with mystics, in a sense the freethinkers of their day, men who, while remaining in the bosom of Tradition, had a more cosmic vision of religion. Centuries of struggle — usually larval, sometimes overt — between doctors of the Law and God's madmen have given much rich material to Persian literature. Many stories and books refer to it, and its roll of martyrs is a long one. And this struggle, essentially between two types of behaviour, was apt for expression on many different levels: in the domain of love, it opposed divine folly to the prudence of reason; on the ethical level, the preacher's good name contrasted with the scandalous misconduct of the mystical libertine; and in the domain of religion, the initiatory path of the sages ran counter to the rigid exoterism of the devotees.

But although historically the mystic, in the broad sense, remained wholly integrated into the religious vision, constituting — with his exoteric counterpart, the theologian — two faces of a single phenomenon, the case was quite different for intellectuals who derived their discourse from a radically different world. This new group, a product of modernity, was a formidable adversary which seemed to have arrived from another mental planet: it thought differently, believed in different values, and reasoned in a way which had no common measure with the premises of the country's culture. In a sense this new group replaced the mystics, who had abandoned centre stage long before, after the decline of the Sufi fraternities.

Between the mystics' world and that of the intellectuals, radical breaks had occurred. Although the mystic — vertiginous paradoxes and all — remained inside the Tradition, the intellectual could only be opposed to it. His *raison d'être* ran counter to established values: his discourse contained important new elements which had no genealogical affinity with the metaphysical underpinnings of the Iranian Islamic world. In it were bizarre, often presumptuous concepts, reeking of heresy and anathema, ideas that overturned all the familiar stereotypes and outlined a world where God, while not entirely absent, played a far less eminent role than usual. For the first time there was talk of criticism: the calling in question of unalterable dogmas, of customs established centuries before. People started to criticize the misdeeds of absolutism, demanding a constitution to limit the sovereign's autocratic powers and protect ordinary subjects against arbitrary whims or changes of mood. An increasingly lively interest was taken in human rights, introducing a subjective element which had no counterpart in the country's juridical-political context.

The tone had already been set by the reformist thinker Mirza Fath Ali Akhundzadeh (1812-78), a Caucasian from Azerbaijan who wrote in Turkish and Persian and whose large output of plays earned him the sobriquet 'the Oriental Molière'. The definitions he gave of key terms such as revolution, philosophy, liberal, thinker, etc, showed the clear influence of the new paradigm of modernity. They were imbued with secular values which directly threatened the twin structures of the régime — the monarchy and the religion:

> Revolution is the specific state which arises when the people has finally had enough of the sovereign. It rebels against him, gets rid of him and sets about legislating on its own account. It also perceives the absurdity of religious beliefs. It revolts against the *ulemas* and forges a new doctrine for itself with the help of rationalist philosophers.[30]

The philosopher is defined as one versed in the rational sciences, who knows the law of causality and no longer believes in miracles, revelation or alchemy. He denies point-blank that angels, demons and djinns exist, and accuses people who cultivate such idiocies of being half-witted. The liberal turns a deaf ear to the threats of religion and takes no interest in subjects which are beyond comprehension or which remain outside the sphere of nature. The thinker is a multi-faceted philosopher full of good sense and imagination, whose writings on politics and society reveal people's virtues and faults with complete impartiality, objectively, without being swayed by affection or hostility.[31]

In a word, the country was being invaded by a whole new jargon, a deeply suspect language inspired by Western social and political philosophies. This aggression by entirely new concepts was terrifying to the defenders of the divine order, especially as Iran was considerably behind Egypt and the Ottoman Empire in absorbing modernity.

Iran has always shrunk from the influence of modernist ideas. It did not experience Western military superiority until the Russo-Iranian war, which ended in a resounding defeat and a humiliating treaty (1828) under which Iran ceded large territories inhabited by Iranians north of the Araxes. There sometimes occur historic defeats which shape the destiny of a people, leaving a wound which is kept open and unhealed by the collective memory of so many painful losses. Persians often talk about the cession of the 'seventeen towns of the Caucasus' with the bitterness of irreparable loss. The esoteric nature of Shiite consciousness, and the relative solidity of the religious institutions anchored in it, helped maintain the 'zones of resistance' which protected the country against the infiltration of revolutionary ideas from the West.

In fact modernism was the work of lay individuals. The mullahs only got involved much later, when they tried to adapt a few chosen modernist ideas to their vision of the world. Probably more flexible and perhaps more open than those of today, the mullahs showed themselves to be capable strategists during the period of the Constitutional movement. But in thus meddling with modernity, they were only bowing to the demands of a period in which modernity appeared to be the epigone of an inexorable fate which it would be futile to resist. The Iranian researcher Hamid Enayat believes that the role of the clergy was underestimated by the nascent nationalist movement because of a certain anti-clerical climate inspired by the extreme views of a sworn enemy of the clergy, Kasravi (1890-1946).[32] While these reservations are justified, Enayat says, when applied to the *ulemas* of the eighteenth and nineteenth centuries, they are no longer valid for those taking part in the Constitutional movement between 1905 and 1911.[33] Unlike the Turkish Constitutional movement (1908-18) which had historical antecedents — half a century of reforms during the period of *Tanzimat* (from 1826) and the demands of the Young Turks (from about 1860) — the Iranian movement sprang from near-virgin territory.

Enayat underlines the decisive advantage given to the *ulemas* in the juridical sphere by the high degree of technical subtlety attained by the Shiite *ulemas* in the science of jurisprudence (*usul al-fiqh*). This development was due partly to centuries of polemic between the *Usuli* and the *Akhbari*. The latter group — strict traditionalists — had been attacked in the eighteenth century by Mohammad Baqer Behbahani, and had subsequently undergone an impressively thorough doctrinal mauling. The moment was thus favourable to the *Usuli*, who made skilful use of the tools of Islamic *fiqh*. We have already said the *Usuli* insisted on the legitimacy of reason and practised *ijtihad* (independent reasoning in the interpretation of Islamic law), in contrast to conservative traditionalists who were distrustful of reason or consensus and encouraged imitation (*taqlid*). Enayat concludes that the political implications of these principles are evident: by backing the authority of reason and promoting *ijtihad*, the *Usuli* helped prepare the Shiite mentality to accept social change.[34]

To tell the truth I do not know whether the authority of reason — and we still need to know what reason, exactly, we are talking about — and the encouragement of *ijtihad* would have been sufficient to start the modernization process. I believe that these tools would have permitted accommodations, rearrangements, adjustments within the *fiqh* itself, but not outside its sphere of action. There were such marked differences between the world of the *ulemas* and the aggressive ideas of modernity that the mere fact of taking an interest would hardly have cleared the way for a real symbiosis; the best that could be hoped for was a sort of compromise built on errors and misunderstandings, with everyone poised to regain his initial position at the first sign of disagreement. The titanic derailment of the mullahs' experiment has now shown clearly, after seventy years of secular experience, that the weapons of the *Usuli*, in the final analysis, were not powerful enough to hold back the landslide, and that the *ulemas* — *Usuli* included — did not really manage to get out of their habitual rut.

In any case, as I have already pointed out, the introduction of modernity was unquestionably the achievement of the secular thinkers who, like those everywhere else in the Islamic world, were aware of the backwardness of Islam and employed all their ingenuity to find compromises and bridges between Islam and modernity.

Neither the *ulemas* nor the traditional literate class were capable of the necessary work of reflection. It had to come from the new intellectuals whose intermediate position made them aware of the full catstrophic scale of the historical time-lapse. The literates and the *ulemas* were the two most immovably fixed educated classes in Persian society. On the one hand was the finicky, precious style of the traditional literary class whose long, obscure, pompous, ostentatiously learned phrases were squandered in empty and trivial flatteries; on the other, the obscurantism of a clergy grimly opposed to all innovation, barricading itself behind an abstruse language and even more impenetrable concepts to arouse passions of the most mindlessly sectarian sort.

In Book II I showed that from the second half of the nineteenth century the theme of *backwardness* obsessed Islamic thinkers more than any other. It was the main platform of the Arabic journal *Al-Urwa al-Wuthqa*, founded in Paris in 1884 by the Iranian al-Afghani and the Egyptian Muhammad Abduh. Like the Turkish and Arab thinkers who had started investigating the causes of the derailment, the reasons for the backwardness and inertia, large numbers of Iranian thinkers of the same period were evolving in the same direction and had similar concerns. Among the most important of these, apart from al-Afghani, were Fath Ali Akhundzadeh (1812-78), Mirza Yusef Khan Mostasharoddowle (d. 1895), Mirza Malkam Khan (1833-1908), Mirza Agha Khan Kermani (1854-96) and Talebof (1834-1911).

There is no need here to go into detail on these authors; suffice it to say that all are more or less liberal thinkers fascinated by the Occident, aware of the gap and anxious to close it. But although all are agreed that the gap exists, the solutions proposed vary from one author to another. Some, such as Akhundzadeh and Mirza Agha Khan Kermani, are openly anti-clerical — even anti-religious in some cases — and favour rapid Westernization on all levels. Kermani is particularly outspoken and spares nobody, especially mullahs whom he accuses of wallowing in useless and sterile scholastic arguments. But despite their virulent tone and the unflattering picture they paint of the country's ambient obscurantism, these attacks stop short of being iconoclastic. Somehow they treat the religious spirit with consideration; they do not go as far as the European Enlightenment philosophers in undermining the foundations of revelation. Criticism is directed against institutions and the people who embody them, not against religion itself.

But others actively seek reconciliation and compatibility. Malkam Khan, a Muslim convert of Armenian origin who ran a review called *Qanun* from London between 1890 and 1898, raises the question of the relationship between modern law and the *Shari'a*. A reformist author (and a freethinker in private), he laid before the Qajar sovereign Nasereddin Shah (1846-96) a set of reform proposals (*daftar-e tanzimat*) based on the Ottoman reforms. The proposals warned the sovereign of the imminent danger of colonial servitude: hence the need for reforms and the establishment of modern law, different from the *Shari'a* and from customary law (*'urf*).

Apart from this adjustment, Malkam Khan favours equality of the two systems, but he specifies that before anything is adopted it has to be adapted to the conditions of the country. The backwardness gap is not caused by religion or any fundamental factor, but by the political system and cultural isolation. To remedy the first of these he proposes positive laws protecting life, liberty, property and security; to overcome the second, he favours the introduction of modern concepts (but adapted to the Islamic mentality). To get these ideas accepted, implicit antecedents should be found in the Quran:

> We have discovered that ideas which were in no way acceptable when they came from our agents in Europe, were immediately accepted with the greatest joy, when it was demonstrated that they were already latent in Islam.[35]

Thus no progress can be made in this direction until it is proved that it is not we who are imitating the Occidentals, but they who are filching our ideas and returning them later in shop-soiled condition. I am not sure whether Malkam Khan's aim of veiling Western philosophies in the immaculate robe of the Quran and the *hadith* was ever achieved. Even supposing that it was, for a time, this incongruous marriage can only have been a most shaky union. All the same, later thinkers have returned to this idea with redoubled energy.

Believers in the equivalence of the two systems were, however, ignoring an important point: the fact that the new spirit contained in modern Western law could only flourish at the expense of the *Shari'a*. To argue that they were not incompatible was not very helpful; it was not possible to retain both at once, given that they were separated by the dead ground of their irreducibility. This could hardly be ignored, even with the best will in the world.

The reaction of the *ulemas* was divided. There were some who, like the intellectuals, sought some kind of compromise; but there were others, aware of the yawning gap between their religion and the innovatory ideas, who adopted a position of brutal opposition. The first were known as 'constitutionalists' and the second as 'absolutists'. But even those sympathetic to change, Kasrawi tells us, acted more out of loyalty to religion than concern for democracy.[36]

Categorical rejection, an absolute *nyet!* to any compromise, was symbolized by Shaykh Fazlollah Nuri, found guilty of being a reactionary and hanged in 1909. In a sense, this rejection remains very important. Although he had played an active part in the early days of the

Constitutional movement, the Shaykh knew that the spirit of the constitution, based on Western philosophies, had no ontological affinity with his religion; that constitutional law (*mashrute*) and divine law (*mashru'e*) were not in the same register and did not derive from the same sources. Men could not be equal before the law, as the new juridical vision required, because Muslims and infidels were not equal before God and did not have the same nature.

The Clergy and the Monarchy

The 1906 constitution was a compromise between the three forces which existed side by side without blending into a coherent whole: the monarchy, the religion, and modernity in its broadest sense. The constitution was an attempt to integrate them more fully. While the first two elements were at least products of the same soil, sharing the blemishes of a long complicity, the last was a new arrival from another world, and therefore somewhat exposed; by the same token, it was the most original and disturbing of the three. Nevertheless the three forces were able to co-operate and managed to establish a sort of balance in the constitution of 1906 and its supplement promulgated in 1907.

The definition of royal power given in article 35 of the supplement is just about as contradictory as it is possible to be: 'The monarchy is a divine trust assigned by the people to the person of the king.' Legitimacy springs from two parallel sources; sovereignty is claimed by both people and God, with the hapless monarch pulled in two directions. In addition, the clergy ensured a decisive role for itself by creating a Council of Theologians, comprising between five and twenty experts, whose job was to ensure that laws promulgated in the representative assembly conformed to the sacrosanct Islamic *Shari'a*. The arrangement was never properly applied, however, and under Reza Shah it fell into disuse. In a sense the Islamic Republic was the clergy's spectacular revenge for this unpardonable affront.

The most convincing theory on balancing the three forces was that of Shaykh Mohammad Hoseyn-e Na'ini (1860-1936), whose *The Admonition and Refinement of the People*[37] is probably the best work written on the subject. Na'ini — well aware of the high stakes and of the contradictory currents dividing the country — opts for limiting the king's powers on the ground that any excess, in whatever form, leads inevitably to tyranny. As the Imamate is absent and we are in the time of Occultation,[38] no sovereign, even the most just, can benefit fully from the innocence which would render him untarnishable. Whence the need to minimize damage by restraining, juridically if necessary, the arbitrary power of the political régime. The régime is a usurper. For in the time of Occultation, all legitimacy ceases to exist on the terrestrial plane and any régime, whatever its tenor, bears by definition the mark of usurpation. Limiting the power of the sovereign through a representative assembly (*majles*) elected by the people is an application of the principle of consultation set out in the Quran. This assembly should be governed by a constitution covering matters which are not mentioned or foreseen by the *Shari'a*. The constitution is not opposed to divine Law; indeed it is complementary to it. Here once again is Malkam Khan's theme of equality between the two systems, also suggested by other Persian and Arab reformists. It has to be admitted that it leads directly to a duality of two different bodies of law, modern secular law and Islamic law; but the contradictions can be greatly reduced by bringing religious dignitaries into the assembly to ensure that new laws are compatible with the *Shari'a*. In any case, the perfect application of the Law of God is not possible until the Advent of the Imam, at the end of Time. Until then there will always be a need for accommodations, arrangements, adjustments. The *ulemas'* flexible attitude towards a monarchy restrained by law, and their acceptance of a secular law harmonized with the Quran, created an atmosphere of compromise which lasted long enough for the clergy to combine forces with secular elements in pursuit of common objectives.[39]

Na'ini's work suggests pretty clearly that the traditional *ulemas* — of course the ideological *ulemas* who appeared later were a different matter — never sought the overthrow of the monarchy. In effect the constitutionalists had taken up the pro-monarchy arguments put forward by jurists in the Safavid period (1501-1722). To quote Mullah Mohammad Baqer, better known as Mohaqqeq Sabzevari (d. 1679):

No time is devoid of the existence of the Imam, but in certain periods the Imam is absent from the eyes of human beings for some reasons and expediencies, but even then the world is prospering thanks to the emanation of His existence . . . Now in this period, when the Master of the Age . . . is absent, if there is no just and judicious king to administer and rule this world, the affairs will end in chaos and disintegration, and life will become impossible for everybody. But it is inevitable, and imperative, for people [to be ruled by] a king who will rule with justice and follow the practice and tradition of the Imam.[40]

In a country like Iran, where royal charisma (*farr-e izadi*) has semi-mystical prestige and is woven into mythology and the genealogy of the ancient Persian sovereigns, the idea of a monarchy was so deeply rooted in collective memory that it was never questioned by traditional elements until the advent of the Islamic Republic. Even the *Fedaiyan-e Islam*, an Iranian fundamentalist version of the Muslim Brotherhood, never dreamed for a moment of getting rid of the monarchy; at most, they wanted to clean up and spiritualize its image. The idea is explicitly present in the manifesto of their leader Nawwab Safavi (1924-56), who was incontestably one of the great intellectual influences on the Islamic Republic. In *The Guide to Truth*[41] he presents his overall vision of the ideal Islamic state, listing the reasons for the creation of such a state and defining the role of the clergy as the ultimate 'Source of Imitation'. He also goes into some detail on the various state institutions, the role of the media and the ministries. His views on the Ministry of Finance display an old-fashioned — one might almost say fairy-tale — view of the economy: 'The model for the Ministry of Finance should be the shop of an apothecary or grocer, who avoids every form of waste and strives to increase his personal fortune.'[42]

Nowhere is there any suggestion of seeking to overthrow or replace the king. On the contrary, the Shah should be more than a puppet: 'The Shah is for society as a father for his family.'[43] The Shah should be a good Muslim and take the first Imam Ali as his exemplary model. He should also attend communal prayer every Friday and on feast-days.[44]

To my knowledge, the traditional clergy never wanted a state where, in the absence of the Imam, there was no sovereign of any kind to absorb the blows of adversity and serve as a cushion or buffer. Indeed the Priest and the King — *Rex-Flamen*, Dumézil would say — were the two poles of Iranian society, were in fact complementary. They were regarded as 'two stones in a single setting'. The fall of the monarchy left religion in an extremely dangerous situation, its representatives committed to a risky adventure, pushed into a game of double-or-quits. Either it would win and emerge profoundly and permanently changed, or it would lose; perhaps lose everything including its skin. With the protective screen of the monarchy removed, religion became the obvious target for all attacks. In my opinion, this spectacular revenge by the *ulemas* was a delayed but extremely violent response to an earlier imbalance caused by Reza Shah's (1874-1944) foundation of the nation state.

The somewhat precarious balance between the three forces (religion, monarchy and modernity)established in the 1906 constitution was upset by Reza Shah in favour of a *monarchy-modernity axis*: he drove religion out of the public domain by depriving it of its two most cherished functions, education and justice. This not only placed all executive, legislative and judicial power in the monarchy's hands, either directly or through the agency of modern institutions like the Ministry of Justice, but enabled the Shah to accelerate the process of secularization by giving preference to modernist influences. Although the mullahs supported some reforms and opposed others, this was not so much for love of liberty as because the measures seemed likely to reinforce or weaken their own privileges. No autonomous solution, independent of religion and monarchy, could take root until the society had freed itself from the tutelage of kings and the equally inconvenient guidance of mullahs. This did not occur in Reza Shah's day, and the present state of things is no more developed.

The Islam which confronts us today is an Islam ideologically marked by the era of revolutions (*Thawra*). It is an Islam which rejects the equality between the modern and traditional systems on which the former constitution of the country was based. It assumes the absolute superiority of Islamic *Shari'a* over all other juridical and social systems; and is thus very different from the more or less critical Islam of the period of renaissance (*Nahda*). What one might call the three pillars of Persia's 1906 constitution — religion, monarchy and modernity — have undergone major mutations. When we scratch the surface of the new Islamic order we see that each of these concepts has been profoundly modified. Modernity is no longer perceived as a rational whole embodying the liberal values (principles of the Enlightenment, classical democracy, fundamental liberties and so on) which once inspired the majority of innovators and reformers in the countries of Islam. Instead it has become a modernity radicalized by revolutionary struggles, debased by totalitarian régimes and above all, in our own cultural environment, disfigured by a pervasive infrastructure derived from the Marxist vulgate, a sort of omnipresent, airborne ideology which has infiltrated the vision of the majority of Islamic thinkers, even the most orthodox.

Shiism itself has diverged from its traditional course. From being an organ of spiritual and moral control, it has now turned into a sort of ultimate oppressive régime, pre-empting the apocalyptic role which, in Twelver Shiite terms, belongs exclusively to the *Mahdi*, the Twelfth Imam who is to bring the cycle of Time to a close. In a way the establishment of an Islamic Republic anticipates the Saviour's messianic task.

The monarchy of course has been wholly eliminated. But an archetype on such a scale, strongly rooted in historical memory, leaves a hole which is not going to be filled in overnight; so the *priest* has been obliged to make himself king, and the Custodianship of the Theologian (*walayat-e faqih*) has been substituted for the imperial charisma of the King of Kings (*farr-e izadi*). To use a parallel with the Indian caste system, this is equivalent to a brahman *coup d'état* against the *kshatriyas* (warriors). But the monarchy has not been eliminated in favour of secularism or some kind of democratic government. On the contrary, one *myth* has been substituted for another, but it is a myth which, in the economy of the symbolic vision of forms, can only function in the presence of its *complement*. In banishing the king, the clergy did away with its own other half. In the process it became fragile and offered itself as fodder to all the demons of temptation. Traditional society has gone lame. A situation in which the priest crowns himself without becoming king is the worst possible solution. The clergy is in the front line. Whatever happens, it will inevitably suffer the irrevocable consequence.

Moreover, the radicalization of religious discourse has pushed Islam over the edge into the most perilous adventures. The mullahs have become the most voracious consumers of every imaginable distortion. From rabid Marxists they have learned the logic of all-or-nothing, class resentment, and above all the anti-imperialist discourse; from the romantic counter-culture of the nostalgics they have acquired slogans reeking with archaism and obsessed with identity; and from their own garden they have harvested a fine crop of emotionally charged ideas, kept repressed in the religious imagination over several decades of secularization. The result is an archaic explosion unprecedented in the history of the country. The mullahs are putting their most unhinged fantasies into effect, giving free rein to their unbridled imagination, whipping the cult of martyrdom from frenzy to paroxysm, reducing timeless myths to their most flatly operational value: and they are innovating in all directions. They have given concrete form to hallucinatory possibilities that once seethed harmlessly in the formless magma of our collective unconscious. In the process they have undermined their own world, emptied Islam of its substance and, avid for survival, in love with destruction, are crudely gambling the spiritual capital accumulated over fourteen hundred years of history. On the outcome of this vast game of poker depend the future of Shiite Islam and the fate of modernity.

Notes

BOOK I: THE SPLIT

1. Quoted by A.K. El Janabi, 'Sur la Culture arabe actuelle', in *Sou'al*, no. 3 (Paris, 1983), pp. 48-50.

2. Quoted by W. Heisenberg, *La Nature dans la physique contemporaine* (Gallimard, Paris), 'Idées', pp. 25-6.

3. Jacques Gernet, *Chine et christianisme* (Gallimard, Paris, 1982), pp. 33-4.

4. Ibid., p. 65.

5. The missionaries referred to Jesus Christ as 'Master of Heaven' to give him a Confucian connotation.

6. Gernet, *Chine...*, p. 277.

7. Ibid., p. 80.

8. Fernand Braudel, *La Dynamique du capitalisme* (Arthaud, Paris, 1985), pp. 19-20.

9. Bernard Lewis, *The Muslim Discovery of Europe* (W.W. Norton & Co., New York and London, 1982).

10. Ibid., p. 51.

11. Ibid., p. 296.

12. Ibid.

13. Jacques Ruffié, *De la Biologie à la culture*, vol. II (Flammarion, Paris, 1983), p. 203.

14. Luc Barbulesco and Philippe Cardinal, *L'Islam en questions* (Grasset, Paris, 1986).

15. Ibid., p. 97.

16. Ibid., p. 146.

17. Ibid., p. 145.

18. Ibid., p. 197.

19. Ibid., p. 214.

20. Ibid., p. 219.

21. Ibid., p. 267.

22. Ibid., p. 116.

23. Ibid., p. 153.

24. Octavio Paz, *One Earth, Four or Five Worlds* (*Reflections on contemporary history*), transl. H. Lane (Carcanet, Manchester, 1985), p. 168.

25. Barbulesco and Cardinal, *L'Islam en questions*, p. 208.

BOOK II: THE ONTOLOGICAL DISPLACEMENT
1. *Pascal's Pensées* (no. 258), transl. H.F. Stewart D.D. (Routledge & Kegan Paul, London, 1950), p. 150.
2. The opening sentence of *Emilius, or a Treatise of Education, translated from the French of J.J. Rousseau, Citizen of Geneva* (A. Donaldson, London and Edinburgh, 1768).
3. Ernst Cassirer, *La Philosophie des Lumières*, p. 173.
4. Sadra is an illustrious example of the 'Persian Platonists'. He is responsible for the revolutionary replacement of the metaphysics of the 'Essences' by a metaphysics of Existence. See H. Corbin, *Histoire de la philosophie islamique* (Gallimard-Folio, Paris, 1986), pp. 467-76.
5. S. Radhakrishnan, *Indian Philosophy* (Allen & Unwin, London, 1962, vol. I, p. 52.
6. See Daryush Shayegan, *Hindouisme et soufisme* (Ed. de la Différence, Paris, 1979).
7. See also R.C. Majunedar (ed.) *The History and Culture of Indian People*, vol. I: *The Vedic Age* (London, 1957); vol. II: *The Age of Imperial Unity* (Bombay, 1960); vol. III: *The Classical Age* (Bombay, 1962); and *The Cultural Heritage of India* (The Ramakrishna Mission), vol. I (1958); vol. II (1962); vols. III and IV (1966).
8. *Encyclopaedia Universalis*, vol. 4 (Paris, 1980), p. 325.
9. Ibid.
10. Ibid.
11. C.P. Fitzgerald, *China: A Short Cultural History* (New York, 1959); Marcel Granet, *La Pensée chinoise* (Paris, 1934); J. Needham, *Science and Civilization in China*, vols. I-IV (Cambridge, 1945-65).
12. Octavio Paz, *One Earth, Four or Five Worlds (Reflections on contemporary history)*, transl. H. Lane (Carcanet, Manchester, 1985).
13. Ibid.
14. Ibid.
15. Octavio Paz, *La Fleur saxifrage* (Gallimard, Paris, 1984), p. 74.
16. Paz, *One Earth . . .*, p. 164.
17. Fernand Braudel, *La Dynamique du capitalisme* (Arthaud, Paris, 1985), p. 91.
18. Ibid., p. 107.

19. John Naisbitt, *The Year Ahead, 1986* (Warner Books, New York, 1985), pp. 21-37.

20. Thomas S. Kuhn, *The Structure of Scientific Revolutions* (University of Chicago Press, Chicago and London, 1962).

21. Ibid., p. 110.

22. Ibid., p. 117.

23. Ibid., p. 119.

24. F. Capra, *The Turning Point* (Flamingo, London, 1984).

25. Octavio Paz, *Conjunctions and Disjunctions*, transl. H. Lane (Arcade, New York, 1990), ch. 3.

26. Ibid., p. 48.

27. Ibid.

28. Ibid., p. 59.

29. Mohammed Arkoun, *La Pensée arabe* (PUF, Paris, 1979).

30. Ali Merad, *L'Islam contemporain* (PUF, Paris, 1984), p. 43.

31. Translated and quoted by H. Pakdaman, *Djamal-ed-din Assad Abadi dit Afghani* (G.P. Maisonneuve et Larose, Paris, 1969), p. 243.

32. Ibid., p. 244.

33. Ibid., p. 288.

34. R. Brunschvig, 'Problème de la décadence', in *Classicisme et déclin culturel dans l'histoire de l'Islam* (G.P. Maisonneuve et Larose, Paris, 1977), pp. 29-51.

35. Ernest Renan had delivered a resounding lecture entitled 'Islamism and Science' at the Sorbonne on 29 March 1883 (published in *Le Journal des débats*), in which he made the categorical assertion that Islam is contrary to the scientific spirit. Al-Afghani's response was fairly restrained.

36. See Quran LXXI, 14: '[When] He created you by (divers) stages (*atwaran*)'; LXXXIV, 19: 'That ye shall journey on from plane to plane (*tabaqan 'an tabaqin*)', *The Koran*, transl. (1930) Mohammed Marmaduke Pickthall (Star pb., W.H. Allen & Co., London, 1989).

37. Arkoun, *La Pensée arabe*, p. 107.

38. Daryush Shayegan, *Qu'est-ce qu'une Révolution religieuse?* (Les Presses d'aujourd'hui, Paris, 1982), p. 230.

BOOK III: THE FIELD OF DISTORTIONS

1. 'Trailing behind' should be understood here not in the chronological but in the ontological sense. A consciousness which is 'trailing behind' means a consciousness which is still close to the earliest myths and realities.

2. Sudhir Kakar, *Moksha, le monde intérieur, enfance et société en Inde* (Les Belles Lettres, Paris, 1985), p. 90.

3. Pérez Galdós, quoted by Octavio Paz, in *One Earth, Four or Five Worlds (Reflections on contemporary history)*, transl. H. Lane (Carcanet, Manchester, 1985), p. 168.

4. Edgard Morin, *La Méthode III, la connaissance de la connaissance* (Seuil, Paris, 1986), p. 190.

5. See Daryush Shayegan, 'Le Retrait des projections et compensations', in Michel Cazenave (ed.), *Cahier de l'Herne, C.G. Jung* (L'Herne, Paris, 1984), pp. 466-73.

6. C.G. Jung, *L'Ame et la vie*, transl. Yves Le Lay (Buchet-Chastel, Paris, 1963), pp. 44-5.

7. Ibid.

8. C.G. Jung, *Problèmes de l'âme moderne* (Buchet-Chastel, Paris, 1960), p. 180.

9. Kakar, *Moksha . . .*, p. 157.

10. Ibid.

11. Michel Foucault, *Les Mots et les choses* (Gallimard, Paris, 1966), p. 13.

12. Martin Heidegger, 'L'Epoque des conceptions du monde', in *Chemins qui ne mènent nulle part* (Gallimard, Paris, 1968), pp. 69-100.

13. Ibid., p. 80.

14. Jose-Guilherme Merquior, *Foucault ou le nihilisme de la chaire*, transl. M. Azulos (PUF, Paris, 1986), p. 139.

15. Ibid., pp. 40-1.

16. Foucault, *Les Mots et les choses*, pp. 32-40.

17. Ibid., p. 39.

18. Ibid.

19. Ibid., p. 47.

20. Ibid., p. 48.

21. Ibid., p. 61.

22. Ibid., p. 62.

23. Ibid.

24. Ibid.

25. Ibid., p. 69.

26. Ibid., p. 89.

27. Ibid., p. 71.

28. Ibid., p. 92.

29. Ibid., p. 29.

30. Ibid., p. 231.
31. Ibid., p. 220.
32. Ibid., p. 323.
33. Ibid., p. 271.
34. Ibid., p. 329.
35. Ibid., p. 319.
36. Ibid., p. 329.
37. Ibid., p. 321.
38. Ibid., p. 329.
39. Ibid., p. 398.
40. Claude Lévi-Strauss, *Race and History* (Unesco, Paris, 1958), p. 35.
41. Ibid.
42. Foucault, *Les Mots et les choses*, p. 179.
43. Merquior, *Foucault ou le nihilisme de la chaire*, p. 73.
44. Ibid.
45. Paz, *One Earth..*, p. 164.
46. Foucault, *Les Mots et les choses*, p. 54.
47. Ibid., p. 55.
48. Lisbeth Rocher and Fatima Cherqaoui, *D'une Foi à l'autre, les conversions à l'Islam en Occident* (Seuil, Paris, 1986), p. 8.
49. Ibid., p. 15.
50. Daryush Shayegan, *Qu'est-ce qu'une Révolution religieuse?* (Les Presses d'aujourd'hui, Paris, 1982), p. 203.
51. Ibid., p. 213.
52. Founder of the Pahlavi dynasty (1926-79).
53. The dynasty which reigned over Iran from 1796 until 1925 and was replaced by the Pahlavis.
54. Ernst Cassirer, *La Philosophie des Lumières*, p. 49.
55. Quoted in Old French by Cassirer, ibid., p. 176.
56. *Le Règne de la critique*, transl. H. Hildenbrand (Editions de Minuit, Paris, 1979), pp. 88-9.
57. Ibid.
58. Ibid., p. 91.
59. Ibid., p. 93.
60. Footnote at the beginning of Immanuel Kant, *Critique of Pure Reason*, transl. N.K. Smith (Macmillan, London, 1933).
61. Interview with Ehsan Naraghi: 'Il faut prendre en compte de plus en plus le rôle de la religion dans la vie politique des nations' (Increasingly,

the role of religion must be taken into account when considering the political life of nations), *Le Monde*, 22 Aug. 1986.

62. Ibid.

63. Reza Alavi, 'Science and Society in Persian Civilization', in *Knowledge: Creation, Diffusion, Utilization*, vol. VI, no. 4 (June 1985) (Sage Publications Inc.), pp. 329-49.

64. See *L'Ethique protestante et l'esprit du capitalisme* (Plon, Paris, 1964), p. 24; and *Economie et société* (Plon, Paris, 1971), III, ch. 6.

65. Daniel Bell, *The Cultural Contradictions of Capitalism* (Heinemann, London, 1975), p. 10.

66. Ibid., p. 11.

67. Ibid., p. 12.

68. Ibid., p. 14.

69. Gholam Hosseyn-e Sa'edi (1935-85), 'Degardisi wa rahayi-ye avareha', in *Alefba*, II (Paris, 1983), pp. 1-5.

70. *Livre de l'autodestruction des philosophes.*

71. Jean-Robert Michot, 'L'Islam et le monde: al-Ghazali et Ibn Taymiyya à propos de la musique (sama')' in *Figures de la finitude*, Bibliothèque philosophique de Louvain no. 32 (Louvain-la-Neuve, 1988).

72. Ibid.

73. Cornelius Castoriadis, *Devant al guerre* (Fayard, Paris, 1980), p. 238.

74. Ibid., pp. 239-40.

75. Milan Kundera, *The Unbearable Lightness of Being* (Faber, London, 1984).

76. Wilhelm Reich, *The Mass Psychology of Fascism*, transl. T.P. Wolfe (Orgone Institute Press, New York, 1946).

77. M.A. Macciocchi, 'Les Femmes et la traversée du fascisme', in *Eléments pour une analyse du fascisme/1*, 10/18 (Paris, 1976), pp. 156-7.

78. Henry Corbin, *En Islam iranien*, vol. IV (Gallimard, Paris, 1978), pp. 37-8.

79. Zeyn al-Abedin-e Rahnema, *Zendegani-ye emam Hosayn* (Amir Kabir, Tehran, AH 1358), pp. 440-5.

80. See Hamid Enayat, *Modern Islamic Political Thought* (Macmillan, London, 1982), pp. 181-94.

81. Ibid.

82. *Wilayat-e Faqih*, quoted in ibid., p. 194.

83. Walter Benjamin, 'L'Oeuvre d'art à l'ère de sa reproductibilité

technique', in *L'Homme, la langue et la culture* (Denoël-Gonthier, Paris, 1971), p. 146.

84. Jean Baudrillard, *America*, transl. C. Turner (Verso, London and New York, 1988), p. 84.

85. Ibid., p. 104.

86. Ibid., p. 29.

87. Ibid., p. 32.

88. Ibid., p. 95.

89. Ibid.

90. Ibid., p. 37.

91. Ibid., p. 101.

92. Ibid., p. 95.

93. Ibid., pp. 78-9.

94. 'Surréalisme', in *Encyclopaedia Universalis*, vol. 15 (Paris, 1980), pp. 575, 578.

95. 'Le Promeneur aboli ou les métamorphoses du troisième homme', in *Babylone*, no. 5 (Paris, 1986), p. 212.

96. Ibid.

97. Ibid.

98. Ibid., p. 213.

99. Charles Gobineau, *Religions et philosophies de l'Asie centrale* (Gallimard, Paris, 1957), p. 126.

100. Ibid., p. 127.

101. Ibid., p. 126.

102. Ibid.

103. Morteza Nejat, 'Roshangari hadaf-e naqashihaye man est', in *Faslname-ye Honar*, no. 6 (Tehran, AH 1363), pp. 242-55.

104. Mir Hossein Mussavi, 'Roshanfekran-e maghruq dar falsafeha-ye gharbi', ibid., pp. 39-49.

105. Reza Davari, 'Honar-e rahmani wa honar-e shaytani, har do dar dowre-ye ma ravaj darand', ibid., no. 2 (Tehran, AH 1361), pp. 46-54.

106. 'Réalisme socialiste', in *Encyclopaedia Universalis*, vol. 13, pp. 1014-16.

107. 'La Question de la technique', in *Essais et conférences* (Gallimard, Paris, 1958), p. 18.

BOOK IV: THE SOCIAL FOUNDATIONS OF THE DISTORTIONS

1. Gustave Le Bon, *La Civilisation des Arabes* (Paris, 1984), pp. 664-9.

2. *The Philosophy of Hegel* (Dover Publications, New York, 1955).

3. Motahhari, a member of the Council of the Islamic Revolution, was murdered in 1979 by an organization called Forghan.

4. *Elal-e gerayesh-e be maddegari* (Reasons for leaning towards materialism), 8th edn (Tehran, 1957).

5. In the third-world countries which were not colonized and therefore possess no Western language (like French in North Africa or English in India), knowledge of languages becomes a merit in itself, an undeniable instrument of power and social progress.

6. A. Laroui, *La Crise des intellectuels arabes* (Maspéro, Paris, 1974), pp. 199-205.

7. Ibid., p. 202.

8. Sadegh Hedayat, 'L'Enterré vivant' in *La Quinzaine* (Paris), 16-31 Jan. 1987, pp. 13-14.

9. Gaston Bachelard, *La Formation de l'esprit scientifique* (Vrin, Paris, 1965), p. 14.

10. Ibid.

11. Ibid.

12. Charles Gobineau, *Religions et philosophies de l'Asie centrale* (Gallimard, Paris, 1957), p. 75.

13. Ibid., p. 76.

14. Ibid.

15. E.M. Cioran, *The Temptation to Exist*, transl. R. Howard (Quartet Books, London and New York, 1987), p. 71 [re-translated after the colon].

16. Ibid., p. 72.

17. *Le Nouvel Observateur* (Paris), 18-24 July 1986, pp. 51-3.

18. Ibid.

19. Ibid., p. 52.

20. Ibid., p. 53.

21. Octavio Paz, *La Fleur saxifrage* (Gallimard, Paris, 1984), pp. 77-8.

22. Daryush Shayegan, 'L'Idéologie en tant que point de rencontre entre deux mondes', in *Science et conscience* (Stock, Paris, 1980), pp. 470-1.

23. *La Dialectique de la raison* (Gallimard, Paris, 1974), p. 51.

24. Theodor W. Adorno, *Negative Dialectics*, transl. E.B. Ashton (Routledge, London, 1950).

25. Max Horkheimer, *Eclipse de la raison* (Payot, Paris, 1979), p. 17.

26. *The Cultural Contradictions of Capitalism* (Heinemann, London, 1975).

27. Charles Gobineau, *Trois ans en Asie* (Ed. A.M. Métailie, Paris, 1980), p. 203.

28. Cioran, *The Temptation to Exist*, p. 68.

29. Legend has it that the Imam Hussein's wife was the daughter of Yazdegard III, the last sovereign of the Sassanid dynasty.

30. *Maktubat-e Mirza Fath Ali Akhundzadeh*, ed. by Sobhdam (Paris, 1984), pp. 9-15.

31. Ibid.

32. A virulent critic of religion and traditional thought. He was murdered by a member of the Fedaiyan-e Islam in 1946.

33. Hamid Enayat, *Modern Islamic Political Thought* (Macmillan, London, 1982), p. 168.

34. Ibid.

35. Quoted by Ervand Abrahamian, *Iran between Two Revolutions* (Princeton University Press, Princeton, N.J., 1983), p. 68.

36. Ahmad Kasrawi, *Tarikh-e mashrute-ye Iran* (Amir Kabir, Tehran, n.d.), p. 259.

37. *Tanbih al-ummah wa tanzih al-milla dar asas wa usul-e mashrutiyyat.*

38. The Twelfth Imam, called the Resurrector, the *Mahdi*, the Master of Time, was occulted at the age of 5 on 24 July 874. During the Lesser Occultation, which lasted until 941, the Imam communicated with his Intermediaries. The death of the last of these ushered in the 'Great Occultation' (*ghaybat-e kobra*) whose end coincides with the expected Advent of the Imam.

39. Hamid Algar, 'Islah', in *Encyclopédie de l'Islam*, new edn, vol. IV (Brill, Leiden, 1978), p. 171.

40. Quoted by Enayat, *Modern Islamic Political Thought*, p. 173.

41. The analytical résumé of this treatise has been translated into French by Yann Richard, 'L'Organisation des *Feda'iyan-e Islam*, mouvement intégriste musulman en Iran (1945-1956)', in Olivier Carré and Paul Dumont (eds), *Radicalismes islamiques* (L'Harmattan, Paris, 1985), pp. 54-66.

42. Ibid., p. 60.

43. Ibid., p. 61.

44. Ibid., p. 62.

Index